Making Peace In and With the World

Making Peace In and With the World:
The Gülen Movement and Eco-Justice

Edited by

Heon Kim and John Raines

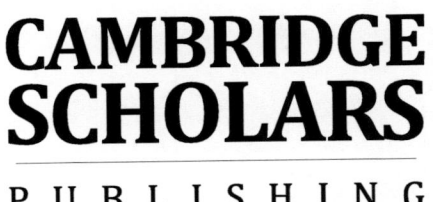

Making Peace In and With the World:
The Gülen Movement and Eco-Justice,
Edited by Heon Kim and John Raines

This book first published 2012

Cambridge Scholars Publishing

12 Back Chapman Street, Newcastle upon Tyne, NE6 2XX, UK

British Library Cataloguing in Publication Data
A catalogue record for this book is available from the British Library

ISBN (10): 1-4438-3567-6, ISBN (13): 978-1-4438-3567-1

TABLE OF CONTENTS

Acknowledgments

I owe my gratitude to many people who have made this volume possible.

My gratitude goes first to the contributors to this volume. With their specialties in diverse fields, they have created a rich and engaging dialogue which took place at the conference at Temple University, Philadelphia PA in November 2010, resulting in this volume. I also appreciate the patience they have shown during the editing process of this volume.

I am deeply grateful to Professor John Raines, the co-editor of this volume. I have been amazingly fortunate to have him as one of my professors and colleagues at Temple University. Just as his insightful guidance opened my intellectual eyes to religious phenomena, he guided this volume with his deep concern, pioneering work, and helpful suggestions.

I wish to mention with immense gratitude Dr. Naci Yazilioglu of the University of Pennsylvania. He has been greater than I could possibly thank him for. His never-failing encouragement did not allow me to be lazy. Particularly, he showed his trust in me to overcome many difficult situations from the preparation of the conference up to this point of the publication of this volume.

I am also indebted to the Department of Religion, Temple University, and Philadelphia Dialogue Forum, the co-sponsors of the conference. Particularly, I am grateful to Dr. Terry Rey, the Chair of the Department of Religion, and Dr. Ismail Kul, a professor of Widener University for their valuable support. Among many members of the Forum that I am indebted to are Dr. Mustafa Koksal, President of the Forum, and Mr. Gazi Ataseven, who never failed to support the publication of this volume.

Last but not least, I would like to express my gratitude for our editors at Cambridge Scholars Publishing, particularly Carol Koulikourdi, Amanda Millar and Soucin Yip-Sou for their genuine supports and understanding throughout the project.

—Heon Kim
East Stroudsburg, Pennsylvania, USA
November 1, 2011

PREFACE

Recently I was asked by a Belgian friend a somewhat sanctimonious question about how shameful it must sometimes feel to be an American: "First Reagan and now the Bush dynasty; given what your country does to the world, it must be very hard to be proud to be an American. Surely there is nothing that you are proud of as an American, right?" Resisting the temptation to say anything about the horrors of the Belgian Congo, I replied, "Well, actually there are things that I am proud of as an American, and none more so than the fact that my country is home to the most diverse Muslim population in the world." He didn't quite know what to say. It is indeed the case that there are Muslims of more national and ethnic backgrounds living in the United States than in any other nation on earth. Together they are a small minority in the US, to be sure, but numbering now several million, Muslims are an increasingly visible and important part of what America is and what America means.

What America means has, of course, always been a heatedly debated question, and the earliest attempts to answer it were crafted right here, in Philadelphia. For one of the most notable and in this case relevant examples, William Penn, a Quaker who had suffered religious persecution in his English homeland, founded the colony of Pennsylvania and its capital city of Philadelphia as a "holy experiment," a place where (white) peoples of diverse (Christian) denominations (Catholics initially excluded) would be free to practice their faiths and have their rights to do so protected by law. Though promoted by a man who himself owned slaves, and bankrolled by an economy fueled by the labor of enslaved Africans on Caribbean plantations, Penn's Philadelphia was the seedbed for the extraordinary religious diversity that we Americans celebrate and cherish today. It's unimaginable that the Quaker would have then foreseen that one of the fruits of his vision would be the extraordinary Islamic diversity of today's American religious mosaic. Yet, here we are today, in Philadelphia, an important center of Islam in North America, discussing the vision of another religious leader who also had to leave his own homeland and settle in Pennsylvania to practice his faith in peace, the influential Turkish Sufi Fethullah Gülen.

It is thus fitting that the impressive scholars represented in this volume gathered in November 2010 in Philadelphia to explore the implications of

Gülen's teachings for "making peace in the world and with the world." It is also fitting that the gathering took place at Temple University, where, especially in its Department of Religion, the study of Islam has enjoyed as long and productive a history as any other institution of higher learning in North America. Since the late 1960s, students from near and far have come here to study Islam, some of them going on to be counted among the leading authorities on the religion in the world today. Over the last five years, in my own classes that cover other topics, I have had Muslim students from Afghanistan, Albania, Bangladesh, Bosnia, Ghana, Egypt, Ethiopia, Indonesia, Iran, Morocco, Nigeria, Pakistan, Palestine, Turkey, Senegal, South Korea, Ukraine, and the United States (and surely I am missing some). Thus when it was proposed that a conference on one of the most influential Islamic thinkers in the world be held here, my reaction was, "Where else?"

Temple's founder, Baptist minister Russell Conwell, envisioned this university as a place where intellectual diamonds could be mined from the under-privileged neighborhoods surrounding its North Philadelphia campus. Arriving in Philadelphia exactly 200 years after Penn and establishing the university two years later, just as Penn probably did not foresee Muslims as part of his holy experiment, Conwell probably did not imagine that some of the diamonds passing through Temple's halls would be Muslims, some of them from North Philly, to be sure, but many others from every corner of the globe. Some of them read Fethullah Gülen in our classes, just as they read William Penn, Russell Conwell, Malcolm X, and Sonia Sanchez. One hopes that in placing their lessons in conversation with everything else that students learn at Temple and in Philadelphia, they leave here empowered, Inshallah, to contribute to peacemaking and to the realization of the university's mission "to create new knowledge that improves the human condition and uplifts the human spirit." That, at any rate, is a central purpose of the book that you are reading today.

—Terry Rey
Philadelphia, Palm Sunday 2011

INTRODUCTION

HEON KIM

Peace has become a key word today. The ongoing warfare and environmental problems alert us to our sustainability in this globalized world. We have observed the twentieth century as a century of war, which opened this millennium with the traumatic 9/11 and continued warfare in many parts of the world. We have also experienced the planetary environmental changes and ecological crisis from global warming to the recent oil spill in Gulf of Mexico and the nuclear crisis in Japan. A warning light of 'the end of nature and humanity' frames our global and local experience and leads us to seek peace today more than any time in history.

This volume cuts through these two problems, and correspondingly addresses two dimensions of peace - making peace between differing human communities and making peace between humanity and nature. The phrase 'eco-justice' in this volume signifies this dual reality, and thereby we hope to offer a unique view that justice in the world must go hand in hand with ecological justice if peace is to be made.[1]

With its dual foci of peace, this volume participates in and adds to two connected academic fields. Social scientists of religion have focused great attention on the dynamics at play in the interaction between religion, human communities and nature, thereby forming a field of religious ecology. Since this volume explores such dynamics, it promises to cast light on religious ecology as well as to provide natural scientific works with considerable theoretical, philosophical and ethical implications. In effect, this volume amounts to the first multidisciplinary, multifocal discussion of the latest addition to Islamic ecology, a field that has been little examined despite the significant number of Muslims who comprise a fifth of the world's population and compared to ecological studies in other religious traditions like Christianity, Buddhism, Daoism and Jainism. Along with religious ecology, this volume corresponds to studies in the

---

[1] For this idea, I am indebted to John Raines' key note speech to the conference held at Temple University in November, 2010, with the title "Making Peace in and with the World: The Role of the Gülen Movement in the Task of Eco-Justice."

interdisciplinary field of 'war and peace.' Since it deals centrally with the question of religion and eco-justice, this volume challenges assumptions of exclusivist religion, religion-oriented violence and the "Clash of Civilizations"[2]—all of which diminish religious values and realities while belittling their contributions to world peace.

Our authors of this volume take Gülen and the Gülen movement as the case study. Muhammad Fethullah Gülen (b. 1941) is a Turkish thinker and one of the most significant Islamic theologians in the contemporary world; the Gülen movement is the fastest growing Islamic civic movement worldwide. A recent survey, *The 500 Most Influential Muslims,* places Gülen as one of the top 50 influential Muslims today and the movement as a global Islamic network. It further names Gülen among those who "affect huge swathes of humanity," and one who "has gone on to become a global phenomenon in his own right."[3] In fact, social scientists from diverse fields in the west as well as in Turkey have produced an accumulated body of studies on Gülen and the movement to form Gülen studies.[4] The Gülen studies have thus far focused on the topics of tolerance, dialogue and education. Despite many implications of these topics, Gülen's contributions to relevant issues of Eco-Justice and ecology were left untouched until the scholarly conference "Making Peace in and with the World: The Role of the Gülen Movement in the Task of Eco-Justice" held at Temple University in Philadelphia in November 2010.

This conference achieved its initial goal, which was to bring together a critical core of scholars from diverse academic fields to examine relevant paradigms and discourses on the theme of religion, peace and the environment with the foci of Gülen and the Gülen movement, and to chart new directions for future scholarly work. The conference proceedings have been carefully scrutinized and selected to produce this volume. The authors here approach related topics from their own academic disciplines

---

[2] By this term, I refer to Samuel Huntington's theory of "Clash of Civilizations." This theory suggests a religiously intrinsic incompatibility between western civilization and non-western civilizations, and foresees inevitable civilizational clashes and wars; see, Huntington, "The Clash of Civilizations," *Foreign Affairs* (Summer 1993): 22-49.

[3] John Esposito and İbrahim Kalın, eds., *The 500 Most Influential Muslims 2009* (Washington, D.C.: Georgetown University Press, 2009). Available online at http://www.rissc.jo/muslim500v-1L.pdf.

[4] See Heon Kim, "The Nature and Role of Sufism in Contemporary Islam: A Case Study of the Life, Thought, and Teachings of Fethullah Gülen" (PhD diss., Temple University, 2008).

to provide readers with a cutting edge study on peace, Eco-Justice and ecology.

In chapter 1, "The Spiritual Crisis at the Heart of the Crisis of Eco-Justice," John Raines provides a framework for this study. To him, Eco-Justice is necessary to save our earthly communities and the earth. Raines defines Eco-Justice as a dual task of global economic justice and global ecological justice, and argues that for that task, we need to begin reconsidering the human place with respect to the natural world and the human relationship to its material possessions. He speculates,

> Too often in world religions the central concern and promise is the well being of the *Self*. Religious beliefs and practices offer this self "Salvation" or "Enlightenment." Thereby the earth, this living environment that embraces and sustains us, is reduced to a material stage, a mere material backdrop upon which the "higher" religious drama of the self is played out. That way of looking at the world (and treating the world as it is looked at) is the spiritual brokenness that lies at the heart of the environmental crisis. The earth is reduced to dead stuff that we humans buy, use and throw away when, in fact, the earth is our home and mother. At its heart the double crisis of global economic justice and global environmental sustainability is a spiritual crisis. For too many of us, salvation becomes an escape from the material world and enlightenment means the cultivation of an elitist individualism. Both fail the task of Eco-Justice. We must find a new way forward.

For consideration of a new way, Raines proposes that research on Gülen's thought and the Gülen movement would provide insight into the ways in which the material world is treated with respect and reverence.

Chapters 2, 3 and 4 discuss what we need to do to make peace among differing human communities. In chapter 2, "Justice and Charity: Contrasting and Complementary Approaches to Creating the Ideal Society," Joseph Stoutzenberger follows up Raines' suggestion on the global economic justice. He underlines Gülen's view that "at the present time half the world is living on two dollars a day, with a billion people surviving on even less."[5] In Gülen's term, this is the "nightmare scenario" of injustices, and to Stoutzenberger, the task of justice is to overcome such injustices.

Chapter 3, "Violence and the Perception of the Other," looks at another aspect of injustice that causes violence. Throughout this chapter, David Grafton argues that one's perception of the other brings about violence. His own lived experience leads him to note religionist and nationalist

---

[5] Fethullah Gülen, *Toward a Global Civilization of Love and Tolerance* (Somerset, NJ: The Light, 2004), 236.

propaganda that construct images of the other as the "evil in our midst." This sort of constructed images of the other results in violence, and unfortunately, this becomes a pervasive tendency within the human psyche that disrupts the identity and value of the other in order to situate and validate one's own position. This tendency is exemplified by, what Grafton calls, the "nameless and faceless Jihadist," who projects violent Islam. The presence of Jihadists and the consequently imagined violent Islam justify Gülen's critique of violence in the name of Islam. Gülen acknowledges the other as part of God's creation, who shares a common human identity with their names and faces. This perception of the other prevents violence and promotes intentional encounter and engagement with the other.

A desirable and fruitful way to engage with the other is in dialogue. As Grafton's chapter indicates, a dialogue between Christians and Muslims must be held in order to maintain peace among closely-interconnected human communities in today's globalized world. In chapter 4, "End Times for These Times: Eschatology and Dialogue for Peace," Walter Wagner suggests a topic that can bring Christians and Muslims into dialogue. In his analysis, the eschatological concept of End Times, which is common to both Christianity and Islam, postulates preparation of the present for the future. It provides a dynamic that pushes present persons toward the future, and a perspective through which the future is anticipated in the present. Examining Gülen's theology of dialogue, Wagner argues that "inter-religious dialogue is a necessity in the process of achieving the realm of peace in the present that anticipates the blessed Hereafter." In this sense, the concept of End Times provides an essential piece of the foundation for Christian-Muslim dialogue and helps develop effective interreligious dialogue, cooperation and influences for justice and peace.

Concurring with Wagner, Karina Korostelina conceptualizes dialogue as a tool for the development of peaceful co-existence between different faith communities. In chapter 5, "Dialogue between religious communities: Gülen's contribution to Eco-Justice," she envisages a dialogue toward the creation of a common identity. A common identity is, in other words, an overarching identity which serves to "resolve contradictions between regions and makes attitudes toward other religious groups more positive, even if they had a long history of offences." Based on this identity, Korostelina looks at our common goal of saving the earth. This goal can be a strong foundation for interfaith dialogue that leads different religions toward peaceful co-existence, and further creates a new common identity of "We-ness" as responsible inhabitants of our earth.

While these four chapters address peace in differing human communities, the remaining four chapters focus on peace between humanity and nature.

With their diverse approaches, the authors of these chapters offer considerable investigations on ecological crisis and religions. In recent decades, a series of scholarly discussions have revealed the contributions of world religions to ecological crisis.[6] Quite contrary to a belief that monotheistic religions - Judaism, Christianity and Islam - sanction humanity to dominate nature, the discussions have disclosed religious teachings on the interdependent relationship between humanity and nature. While corresponding to these discussions, our chapters uncover a new dimension from the perspective of peace and eco-justice.

Jon Pahl, in chapter 6, "Sacred Space and a Coming Religious Peace in the Thought of M. Fethullah Gülen, and in the Hizmet Movement," introduces a concept of sacred space of nature. He marks Gülen's teaching that "nature is much more than a heap of materiality or an accumulation of objects: It has a certain sacredness, for it is an arena in which God's Beautiful Names are displayed."[7] In Pahl's examination, this teaching has implanted a concept of sacred space of nature into the Gülen movement. Metaphors like light, water, planet, jihad and love, which Gülen uses to describe divine presence and the ideal relationships of different religious people to God and to one another, represent a nature-centered worldview. This worldview reserves the sense of nature as sacred space at the heart of the movement.

A compelling aspect of humanity's interdependent relationship with nature is examined in chapter 7, "Fethulleh Gülen and Eco-Justice: From Genesis 1:28 and Qur'an 2:30 to Platonic *ergon* and Aristotelian *harmonia*." In this chapter, Ori Soltes comparatively analyzes biblical and qur'anic passages regarding human-human and human-natural world relations from the perspective of eco-justice. A particular theological point that Soltes notes is a concept of vice-regent or stewardship over the earth. The qur'anic definition of humankind as being God's appointed vice-regent on the earth is often interpreted as human dominion or subjection over nature. Opposing to this interpretation, Soltes discusses Gülen's emphasis on "If humanity is the viceregent of God on earth... then the Divine Being that has sent humanity to this realm will have given us the right, permission and ability to discover the mysteries imbedded in the soul of the universe... to be the representatives of characteristics that belong to Him, such as knowledge, will and might."[8] This meaning of

---

[6] See for instance, *The Religions of the World and Ecology* series published from 1997 to 2003 by Harvard University Press.
[7] Gülen, *Toward a Global Civilization of Love and Tolerance*, (Somerset, NJ: The Light, Inc., 2006), 313.
[8] Ibid., 204.

human vice-regency necessitates the human act of caring for the world as opposed to humanity's free exploitation of the world.

Heon Kim takes up further the concept of vice-regency. In chapter 8, "Self in and with Others in Gülen's Thought: A Practice of Religious Ecology," he considers the human vice-regency relationship with nature as a central part of Islamic ecology. Kim first presents "the separation thesis between self and others." This thesis refers to otherization of nature, which sees nature not as an organic part of human self but as a mechanical other. Eventually it justifies human exploitation of nature as an object for human benefit. Attributing this thesis as a paradigmatic root of the ecological crisis, Kim parallels it with Gülen's thought, which defines humanity as a mutually interdependent unity of self and other and as an object of love, tolerance and dialogue. In this context, Kim discusses human relationship with nature, centering on the concept of human vice-regency. In Gülen's "love-centric worldview," the duty of humanity as God's vice-regent is to love and care for nature to preserve it as a divine book. Kim presents this view as an ontological basis and moral principle of the nature-human relationship for a discussion about peace in and with the world.

In chapter 9, "The Gülen Movement: Cultivating Eco-Justice Through Education and Self-Refashioning," Margaret Rausch examines to what extent Gülen's vision of peace is embodied in the Gülen movement. Her examination is based upon in-depth interviews with seven men and women affiliates of the movement in the US. The interviews lead Rausch to argue that through a self-refashioning process the affiliates have embodied such virtues as altruism, humility and compassion for humanity and all of creation, and these virtues in turn provide them a new mindset and systemic framework, in which their activities and practices promote dialogue, harmonious co-existence, and peace.

PART 1:

MAKING PEACE BETWEEN DIFFERING HUMAN COMMUNITIES

THE SPIRITUAL CRISIS AT THE HEART OF THE CRISIS OF ECO-JUSTICE

JOHN RAINES

What is Eco-Justice and why should we pursue it? To answer that question let me begin with a puzzle. What's wrong with saying, "we should take better care of the earth?" Because speaking that way we seem to be autonomous beings outside The Great Livingness that enfolds and supports us, as if we should "decide" as outsiders that we should take care of The Living World that at each moment is, in fact, already taking care of us.

Think what it means for us to breathe. We take in oxygen and breathe out carbon dioxide. After these millions of years of animals breathing, how is there any oxygen left? It is because of photosynthesis—all those grassy and green things out there that take in our carbon dioxide and give us back oxygen. We humans breathe only because we are part of a living, breathing world. And that living environment was there with its oxygen millions of years before our species made its evolutionary entrance—awaiting us and ready to welcome us. It is the living environment that takes care of us, not we who take care of it! What we as a species owe the environment is justice—a just recognition of what we depend upon and therefore owe. And that is why in these essays we talk about ECO-JUSTICE.

There is a second reason. Everywhere in the world today, in every nation, and also between the nations of the global North and the global South, inequality is growing. Take for example the growing inequality within my own country. For the past forty years inequality of income and of wealth in the United States has vastly increased. According to Census data, the percentage of U.S. total income in 1976 that went to the top 1 percent of American households was 8.9 percent, but by 2007 that had increased to 23.5 percent. Between 1979 and 2008 the top 5 percent of American families saw their real income (adjusted to taxes and inflation) increase by 73 percent; while over the same period the bottom 20 percent saw a *decrease* in real income of 4.1 percent. If we talk about wealth (which besides income includes real estate, mutual funds, stocks and bonds and retirement accounts), in 2007, according to the Federal Reserve Board, the richest 1 percent of U.S. households owned 33.8 percent of the nation's private wealth. That's more than the combined wealth of the bottom 90 percent! For forty years our country has become more and more divided into *those who have more* and *those who have less.* And what we are talking about here is not just income or wealth, we are talking about power and the use of that power to influence social legislation. Nowhere is this made more evident than in the Bush tax cuts (recently renewed by the Obama administration), where 25 percent of the tax money saved went to the top 1 percent of the tax payers.

Why is this happening? Why are the vast majority of our citizens losing out? Put simply, capitalism has gone global and abandoned its national base. We may call it "runaway capitalism!" First it ran away from the workers of the older industrial nations. For example, beginning in the 1970s American capitalism went global and invested heavily in the electronics and steel industries in Japan and South Korea. But here's the truth, as soon as workers in those countries demanded fair pay, runaway capitalism took those jobs to China (electronics) and Brazil (steel). Workers in America first, but then workers in Japan and South Korea saw their factories close.

This pattern of growing inequality within nations makes itself evident in places we often refer to as "modern miracles of development." Take China. The government there recently increased the minimum pay to $175 per month. In terms of factory workers we find the average yearly income is $3,200. Are there new millionaires, are there new and elegant shopping malls, are there traffic jams in Chinese cities—yes! But the average worker in China can't afford to buy the computers or television sets, or even the designer shoes and clothes that he or she is making. A vast abyss of inequality has opened. Nations of the world are becoming more and more unequal.

Then there is the growing inequality *between* nations, mostly of the global North and global South. Take the case of international debt. Today, each year more money pours out of Africa to the North in terms of debt repayments than flow from North to South as international aid. And there is an irony when the North (especially the U.S.) sends food aid to the starving populations of the global South. The irony is this: the end result is that our federally subsidized corn and wheat find a use but only by destroying the market position of local farmers in the global South, thus cementing in patterns of dependency.

Or take the case of oil-rich Nigeria which sells its oil to the energy voracious North at the expense of polluting its own coastal estuaries and depleting the fish and fowl reserves local populations depend upon. Pesticides forbidden in Europe and North America because of the negative health effects on farm workers are used with abandon in Mexico, Brazil and Africa.[1]

Here we see how economic injustice is tied intimately to ecological injustice. Put simply, runaway capitalism will run wherever it has to run to escape well paid workers but also to escape nations that enforce strong environmental protections laws, and that is why we talk about Eco-Justice. Both global economic justice and global ecological justice is what we talk about because they are two sides of the same coin.

Let me paint you a picture that illustrates this brave new world. In your mind's eye see this: global capitalism has wings but no feet, and we humans have feet but no wings—that is, we humans are confined to living in local communities. That is the only place we can live—in local tax systems, local school systems, local systems of water and waste disposal, local systems of electricity and housing production.

Let me translate that picture of wings and feet into the way in the contemporary world we grow and sell food in this new global system. In the global South in the past 40 years, millions of acres of land have been taken out of production for local appetites—food such as rice and maze, the only food the poor can afford—millions of acres have been transplanted with winter fruits and vegetables for people in the global North who can afford to pay more, and thus increase the profits of global food corporations. The logic which steered the production of food was for millennia the logic of local hunger. No longer! Today, food follows money and flies through the air or travels the oceans. The logic of food is not the hunger of humans but the hunger of corporations for profits. If you live in the United States today your average supper has traveled 1,300 miles to get to your table. We can and do pay for those miles; but those miles leave the poor and their hunger behind.

The result is that 1 billion and perhaps as many as 2 billion of us—almost $1/3^{rd}$ of our human species—lives in what the United Nations calls "Absolute Poverty." This is a New Kind of Starvation, a starvation not caused by natural disaster, a starvation not caused by inadequate food

---

[1] The best work on global inequality is by Branko Milanovic, *Worlds Apart: Measuring International Inequality* (Princeton, NJ: Princeton University Press, 2007). See also Michael Yates, *Naming The System: Inequality and Work in the Global Economy* (New York: Monthly Review Press, 2003). See also Jeffery Faux's *The Global Class War* (Hoboken, NJ: John Wiley & Sons, Inc., 2006). On global inequality and its causes see also Joseph Stiglitz, *Making Globalization Work* (New York: W.W. Norton and Co., Inc., 2006).

production. There is plenty of agricultural productive capacity to feed all six and a half billion of us and feed us well.[2] This new starvation is caused by the fact that poor people make poor customers for the corporate global food system. The result of that is vividly portrayed in our modern world so strangely divided, we could say grotesquely divided into the starved and the stuffed.

Let us return to that picture of wings and feet. Runaway capitalism not only runs away from well paid workers and nations that enforce strong environmental protection laws, it also runs away from the hungry poor of the global South. To address successfully this dual violation of Eco-Justice, what we need to do is to put "feet" back on global capitalism, slowing money down so it serves the well being of humans who necessarily live in local communities. How can we do that? The global instruments are already there. They are the International Monetary Fund, the World Bank and the World Trade Organization. Right now they are driven by the logic of runaway capitalism. But as the crisis of Eco-Justice persists, a new politics will begin to appear, a new understanding of how we humans must construct a fundamentally new way to steer our future together on planet earth. The International Monetary Fund, the World Bank, the World Trade Organization are human creatures and humans can recreate them to serve higher moral purposes than the short term profits of private corporations. And there is a politics for that to happen as I will argue in a moment.

There are important resources in the moral reasoning of both Christianity and Islam for defining and defending such moral purposes. In Christian medieval thought and practice the taking of interest on loans (usury) was strictly forbidden because it put all the risk upon the borrower. Similarly in Islam, *riba* (taking interest on a loan) is prohibited. Both traditions recognize that economic activity needs to be held accountable for moral purposes that surpass private profit.

This heritage within Islamic thought bears directly upon the issue of Fethullah Gülen and his *hizmet* or "service" movement. In his teaching and writings, Gülen has addressed deeply and with insight how the material world is treated by Islam with respect and even reverence. There are generative roots in his thought for the task of Ecological Justice. This will be made clear in other essays in this collection. However, I am less aware of a systemic analysis of how power and privilege work in the capitalist world system to advance and protect elitist interests and advantages. Still

---

[2] These claims on the global food crisis are documented in The United Nations Food and Agricultural Commissions' report on "The New Food Insecurity," August, 2008.

his insistence that religion needs science, just as science needs religion, opens the door to the critical social sciences and their structural analysis of Neoliberal Capitalist "Development." This will help the Gülen Movement address that other side of the Eco-Justice Crisis, namely the crisis of economic justice in a world becoming ever more divided into a powerful international elite and the vast majority who do not belong to that elite and have their voice and interests erased from the discourse of international economic policy decisions.

There is an entrance into such a systemic analysis already in practice in the Gülen Movement. It is this: in 1996, members of the Movement established an interest-free bank (following the Islamic prohibition against *riba*) and in 2006 changed the name to Bank Asya. As of July 2007 that bank had 117 domestic branches, and states its two fundamental purposes "to develop new interest-free banking products" and "to take products that are already being offered at conventional banks and adapt them in such a way as to fit into the system of interest-free banking."[3] The implications of this practice upon the casino-like financial practices dominating global capitalism are indeed radical. That fact needs to be systematically explored by Muslim intellectuals and economists, which would add an important voice to those of us who, as Christians, are highly critical of the elitism and spreading inequality of global Capitalist "Development."

***

I need to explain what I mean by "casino-like." It adds a new feature to the older runaway capitalism. Today, the vast majority of international financial transactions have nothing to do with things made in factories or harvested from fields or rendered in services. Instead, money now mostly makes only more money. It creates no jobs, increases no productive capacity. It is dedicated to pure speculation—thus the word "casino." Read this set of amazing statistics. In 2002 (and it has gotten worse since) worldwide speculative transactions hit an incredible 1,122.7 trillion US dollars. Yes, that's right: one quadrillion, one hundred and twenty two trillion and 700 million dollars. Here's what is crucial. That total was 34.76 times the 32.2 trillion dollars of transactions in goods and services— i.e., the real economy! (Stop. Read that again and think what it means.)[4]

---

[3] Filiz Baskan, "The Political Economy of Islamic Finance in Turkey: the role of Fethullah Gülen in Asya Finans," in *The Politics of Islamic Finance,"* ed. Henry and Wilson (Edinburgh: Edinburgh UniversityPress, 2004).

[4] These statistics are taken from the French Economist, Francois Morin, *Le Mur de l'Argent* (Sueil: The Wall of Money, 2006). Morin is a Professor of Economics at

The Western Christian moral tradition, whether Catholic or Protestant, argued that private property (including investment capital) was morally legitimate only because and in so far as it "served the common good." But in casino capitalism financial transactions have been completely removed from the commons, from the real economy, and have instead been radically privatized. One way to begin to correct this is to create a new international tax on these speculative transactions and so begin to recover lost revenues for public purposes. Such revenues could become a source of what economist Joseph Stiglitz calls "global greenbacks," a source of development investment for poorer countries independent of The International Monetary Fund and the World Bank, dominated as they are by wealthy countries and their interests. In 2010, Spain and France suggested such a tax, but the idea has not generated widespread notice or support.[5]

Imposing such a tax would go a long way toward tipping the balance of international investments back toward local communities and the humans that necessarily live in such communities. It would begin to put "feet" back on global capitalism, bringing it down to earth where it belongs.

The idea that global capitalism could be morally disciplined to serve the well being of humans living in local communities seems farfetched. A sense of realism predicts that powerful interests will use their power to block that move. So let me make a rash prediction. As the global crisis of Eco-Justice persists and even deepens, and as the protest movements against those injustices continue to grow and become transnational in connections, at some point in all of that there will be a sudden change. CEOs and stock holders of major multinational corporations will begin to sense this change and say: "Okay, as long as there are effective international enforcements that disciplines my competition, forcing all of us to play by the new rules of Eco-Justice, then I am with you. Why? Because I have grandchildren and I want to leave to them a world that works!" When that happens, change that previously seemed impossible will come like an avalanche.

But for that happy day to come, there must be one other change, a change in our religious orientation. Yes, this double crisis of Eco-Justice draws us into a deeper dimension of crisis, because the crisis of Eco-Justice is at its heart a spiritual crisis.

---

the University of Toulouse and a member of The General Council of The Bank of France. He argues that 50 percent of the daily trading done in New York and London is done by hedge fund managers.

[5] See http://business.financialpost.com/2011/09/28/eu-proposes-transaction-tax/

Too often in world religions the central concern and promise is the well being of the *Self.* Religious beliefs and practices offer this self "Salvation" or "Enlightenment." Thereby the earth, this living environment that embraces and sustains us, is reduced to a material stage, a mere material backdrop upon which the "higher" religious drama of the self is played out. That way of looking at the world (and treating the world as it is looked at) is the spiritual brokenness that lies at the heart of the environmental crisis. The earth is reduced to dead stuff that we humans buy, use and throw away when, in fact, the earth is our home and mother. At its heart the double crisis of global economic justice and global environmental sustainability is a spiritual crisis. For too many of us, salvation becomes an escape from the material world and enlightenment means the cultivation of an elitist individualism. Both fail the task of Eco-Justice. We must find a new way forward.

I will speak only for my own tradition, Western Christianity. And I will ask, where do the steeples on our churches point us? And why do they point us there? Steeples point us up and away from the ground that holds them up. Steeples witness to a profound lack of connectedness, a lack of gratitude to the material creation that at every moment nurtures and sustains us. What are we fleeing from when we follow those steeples and in our hearts and minds flee the earth?

I think we fear and flee the mortality we share with all other living things. We fear and flee death.

But note this and note it well. Without death we humans as a species would never have evolved, would never have arrived here on planet earth. Without death we humans would not be.

Here, religiously speaking, is where we Christians must take our hearts and minds. God used and continues to use evolution to create and recreate life on earth. Yes, that is how it happened and is still happening even as you read these words. Beginning billions of years ago with simple one-celled life forms in the ocean depths, that is where the story began. Then, over vast time, life evolved to become more and more diverse and more and more complex in its organic base. In that story of life evolving, death is not some punishment. Death is not the opposite or the end of Life. Rather life and death are dance partners of evolution where life takes death into itself and keeps life alive, always changing and still evolving. It's a different kind of Good Friday and Easter story, where life keeps itself alive by using death for the end and purposes of life-evolving.

Let me dare for a moment to do some theology. Creation, I wager, is not something that happened back then and now is finished. That would make the world dead. The Creator and Creation are in fact not separate, one preceding the other, but should be seen and understood as one and the same, joined together as Cosmic Creativity. It is Spirit-filled Matter, star dust blown into the future universe some 14 billion years ago, a cosmic process that is still unfolding. And we humans are a part of all that, indeed a very special part.

If we imagine that story of 14 billion years of cosmic unfolding, if we imagine all that in terms of a bookcase and volumes in that bookcase, there would be 39 volumes. Each volume would have 400 pages, and each page would represent 1 million years. We humans would appear only in the last volume, on the last page and only in the last line. That seems like such a humiliation! But think again! The magic and wonder is that I can say what I just said, and you understood it!

The evolutionary biologist Theodosius Dobchanzky saw the meaning of it all. In his book *Mankind Evolving,* here is what he said:

> "The most important point in Darwin's teachings was, strangely enough, overlooked. Man [!] has not only evolved, he is evolving. This is a source of hope in the abyss of despair. In a way Darwin has healed the wound inflicted by Copernicus and Galileo. Man is not the center of the universe physically, but he may be the spiritual center. Man and man alone knows that the world evolves and that he evolves with it. By changing what he knows about the world man changes the world that he knows; and by changing the world in which he lives man changes himself. Changes may be deteriorations or improvements; the hope lies in the possibility that changes resulting from knowledge may also be directed by knowledge. Evolution need no longer be a destiny imposed from without; it may conceivably be controlled by man, in accordance with his wisdom and his values."[6]

In these words we find hope for the future, but also terrible judgment if we fail to act upon what we know. Today, tomorrow and the day after we live without excuse.

How strange and wonderful that Cosmic Creativity should bring forth here on planet earth an autobiographer of Cosmic Process, a Story-Teller who begins to tell the Larger Story of which our human story is a part. Yes, we humans are becoming a place (we may hope there are many other such places in the universe) where God wants the Story of Cosmic Creativity to be told. And once we begin to tell that story well and accurately, we humans who are Christians will take our steeples and in our imagination turn them upside-down, and thereby return honor and

---

[6] Theodosius Dobzhansky, *Mankind Evolving* (New Haven: Yale University Press, 1962), 226.

gratitude to planet earth which gives us life—in the place where God intended and prepared for us to find life. And when our imagination of hope turns back to earth, we can use our talent for cosmic story- telling to tell us what we need to do, and the knowledge of how to do it.

Life evolving, the life God intends for us, is always and everywhere a yeasty Community Of Life, an immensely complex and meaty interdependency—a vast organic WE. That story is told wrongly when it is told as a Story of Individual Escape, when it is told as a story of Salvation into some spiritual elsewhere, or of elitist Enlightenment and Liberation. The real story is a story of unfolding mutual interdependence—of humans needing and depending upon one another in a life that is always a *life-together*, and of all humans together depending upon the intimate embrace of the Living Environment that at every moment of our individual lives, but also of our collective lives, sustains and nurtures us.

Here, at the end of my reflections, let me return to the same idea as I began. Why is it a mistaken way of speaking to speak about "the environmental crisis?" Because the environment is in crisis only because we humans, and especially we well to do humans, are in crisis in relationship to the environment. The crisis is ours, we made it and we must undo it.

Confession, it is said, is "good for the soul." So let me end my remarks with a confession.

My generation has failed.

We have failed to prevent the two great moral crises that haunt our era and threaten the future. One is the growing inequality within all nations and between the nations of the global North and the global South, and all that means for the precarious future of democratic governance. The second failure of my generation is our inability to discipline our lifestyles and our economic institutions to the task of environmental sustainability. My generation now puts this world into the hands of the younger generation. It is our bitter patrimony.

Still, as Abraham Lincoln once said to his generation, "We must disenthrall ourselves, we must think anew and act anew" and thereby save the future. In the end, my generation shares the same destiny with you younger folks, for both of us, our unborn grandchildren and great grandchildren await our action or our inaction. And surely it is they, not we, who will have the final say and judgment about how we understood and lived our lives.

VIOLENCE AND THE PERCEPTION
OF THE OTHER

DAVID D. GRAFTON

Using a personal experience as a victim of the 2004 Taba terrorist attack in Egypt, this chapter will explore how communal pressures to understand religious and national violence validates one's own status and position and disrupts our ability to see members of another faith community or nation as a creation of God. Constructing images of the Other has been an important part of religious and nationalist propaganda from time immemorial. Constructing an image of the "evil in our midst" is well documented and will be reviewed. Yet, it is also a pervasive tendency within the human psyche to make sense of communal discord and violence by creating easy categories and answers that disrupts the identity and value of another human being. Characterizations and falsification of members of other faith traditions become an easy way to explain actions and validate one's own position. Using Fethullah Gülen's critique of terror in the name of Islam, the chapter will argue that religionists must monitor their own personal, social, ethnic, and nationalist agendas through intentional encounter and engagement with the Other in order to recognize the Other as a creation of God.

Taba 2004

In October 2004, while living in Egypt where I was teaching, my family and I decided to take a short holiday to the Red Sea resort of Taba. Not only was it the term break for my children's school, but also it was the Sixth of October – one of the Egyptian National holidays. In addition, it was Succoth, the Jewish Festival of the Booths, and a National Holiday in Israel. Hundreds of Israeli tourists had crossed the border from Eilat into Taba. That particular weekend the Taba Hilton was packed with unsuspecting tourists.

After our first day of snorkeling on the Red Sea under the hot Egyptian sun of October, we had a memorable dinner of fish and rice before getting our three small children up to our fifth story hotel room to bed. No sooner had we dropped off to sleep when an explosion abruptly awakened us. The large window next to our bed shattered and the frame blew over top of us. In what seemed like a frozen moment of time, the emergency lighting was diffused by dust and smoke that hung in the air.

After we determined that our children were alive, we quickly made our way through the rubble out of the room. In the dark hallway I turned left toward one of the two stairways at each end of the hotel. However, instead of a doorway leading to the stairs, I gazed out into the open night sky. There were no stairs, just a large gaping hole. The Taba Hilton and its guests had just been the victims of a car bomb explosion that killed at least 34 and wounded at least 105 innocents.[1] The dead included Egyptians, Russians, Britons, and Israelis. The perpetrators of this act of terrorism were later acknowledged as an unidentified Islamic Palestinian group.

Although my family and I made it out of the hotel alive, with only minor lacerations, my six-year-old daughter's leg was bleeding due to a wound she received from shrapnel in the explosion. It was several hours before we were evacuated from that site to another local hotel. All I remember from that time was my daughter being carried to a couch in the main lounge of that hotel where she was attended to by a young doctor who introduced himself as Ahmed, and assisted by a young couple that appeared out of nowhere. The young woman was a muhajibat, a veiled Muslim woman.

While that event was certainly life changing for my family and me, it was an event unfortunately like too many other religiously and politically motivated acts that afflicts our world. It is blind violence that seeks to de-personalize "the Other." I, as an American carrying my blue passport, was a nameless and faceless "Other" who was guilty by association of belonging to a government that, according to some, facilitates violent occupation and had just executed a violent invasion of Iraq. The perpetrators of that act were nameless and faceless "Others" who have been called terrorists. And yet, in this particular geo-political event in which I was caught, the only two people that I have any cognizant memory of are those who provided acts of kindness and mercy to me and my family; Ahmad and a nameless muhajibat. I know nothing more of them. I could choose to define Islam through the act of those terrorists who changed my life. Or, I could choose to define Islam through the acts of those two individuals who tended to my daughter.

---

[1] "Death Toll Rises," BBC News Service, October 9, 2004, accessed October 25, 2010, http://news.bbc.co.uk/2/hi/middle_east/3728436.stm.

As a victim of terrorist violence it could be understandable to envision the attackers as inhuman and evil perpetrators of brutality. How much more so for a community or nation to respond to violence perpetrated against it in a similar manner? Unfortunately, it is often the case that societies and nations respond to communal crisis by dehumanizing the "Other" (whoever that "Other" might be; either another nation, culture, or minority community within the state) in order to return their society to "normalcy." Societies often undertake dehumanizing choices to reduce other human beings to a nameless, faceless "Other." It is the "Other" who fulfills a role within a meta-narrative, or "myth," of a particular society that justifies violence against such evil. In order to disengage from this cycle of violence driven by a constructed and created "Other," societies must look inward rather than outward for solutions. Fethullah Gülen's views on Terrorism prove to be a helpful way forward in the face of inter-communal anxiety and violence.

Disruption of Seeing the Other

Politically or religiously motivated acts of communal violence and the desire to retaliate against those who perpetrate such acts of violence enable the dehumanization of the "Other." Rather than seeing the violent "Other" as a human being involved in particular historical conditions that have given rise to violence, it is easier to create our own identity of the "Other" for which we might validate our own positions of security or power, or so that we might psychologically rationalize our feelings of the desire to retaliate.

In the normal course of life, ethical decisions and actions are made within a morass of exigencies. The human being is constantly faced with making ethical choices in the midst of any number of complicating factors. Of course, ideological, philosophical, spiritual and religious meta-narratives do provide guidance for such decisions. Yet, in the act of politically or religiously motivated violence – either as a perpetrator or a victim – communities often seek to simplify the ethical complications and provide clearer validations for one's own positions over and against the "Other." Justice and security for the sake of the common good of any one particular society are often the most prominent rationalizations for national or global violence.

Carl von Clausewitz's historic work, *On War* [Dom Krieg] (1832) describes the origins and prosecutions of war in terms of a rational duel between two parties. The parties have made calculated decisions about their reasons for either engaging in or responding to the duel. And yet, he recognizes:

> ... even the most civilized nations may burn with passionate hatred of each other.We may see from this what a fallacy it would be to refer the War of a civilized nation entirely to an intelligent act on the part of the Government, and to imagine it as continually freeing itself more and more from all feeling of passion . . .[2]

Thus, even a calculated and rational duel may have its origins or causes in some irrational act, some mistaken interpretation of events, or any number of other unreasonable factors. To convince and involve other parties in the justification of this duel may then only magnify those unreasonable, irrational, or mistaken factors. The articulation of an argument for undertaking violence toward another nation or another community requires a clear articulation of "just cause" through *propaganda*. Although often used pejoratively, the definition need not be so. Propaganda is the public articulation of policies and directives for objective purposes. Yet, for a society to be moved to violence it must be convinced and see the justification for taking up arms against an enemy. In such campaigns, exigencies, qualifications, or obfuscations of the issue do not convince. Rather, there must be compelling and clear reasons for a society to undertake violence. And in such cases, the "Other" must be constructed and imagined in such a way as to provide a clear directive to move the public.

While it is one thing to speak about violence against a distant enemy, it is another to construct and imagine that enemy within one's own borders. Phillip Cole, in his 2006 work *The myth of evil: demonizing the enemy*, argued that societies have the need to look for a person, or people, or an event that will play a "mythological" part opposite of its own role on the great stage of world history.[3] Cole reviewed the public responses to the witch-hunts of New England in the 17th century, the vampire-hunts in Eastern Europe of the 18th century, and the anti-Semitism of Europe as social phenomena. In these cases, anxieties were placed not on another nation or population outside the borders of these communities. Rather, fear was placed upon a particular subset within the nation. For Cole, the fear of the "Other" community was generated by the fear of "their ability to pass among us undetected, to appear to be part of humanity but to be secretly

---

[2] Carl von Clausewitz, *On War* (London: K. Paul Trench, Trubner, and Co. Ltd., 1911), 3-4.
[3] Phillip Cole, *The Myth of Evil: Demonizing the Enemy* (Westport, Conn: Praeger, 2006), 23.

scheming its destruction. The person sitting next to you . . . could be a witch or a vampire."[4]

Cole's thesis is borne out by another study. Panikos Panayi's *The enemy in our midst* (1991) is a study of the image of Germans expatriates living in Britain during World War I. Utilizing newspapers and journals, as well as popular novels published during the War, Panayi argues that "spy fever" overtook the British public, and that publications whipped up a hysterical fear that German aliens "might commit acts of sabotage" in their midst.[5] For example, the novelist William Le Queux, published several novels dealing with the fear of German spies, including *German Spies in England* (1915), *The Spy Hunter* (1916), *Number 70, Berlin: A Story of Britain's Peril* (1916), and *The Bomb Makers* (1917). All of these novels contributed to a public hysteria and further fueled anti-Germanism. Panayi concludes that it was the public reinforcement of such hysteria through these publications that contributed to government polices, which either incarcerated or repatriated Germans living in Britain.

In October 1914 an op-ed piece in the London *Times* wrote "No German living in this country, but retaining any feeling of affection for his own, can help sympathizing with her cause and wishing it success. If opportunity offers to help her he will take it."[6] In addition, the daily papers printed numerous "letters to the editor" feeding on this fear: "I *know* I traveled in a bus with two German spies today, and it was such an awful feeling as if a dark shadow was present."[7]

Cole has argued, that in portraying the "Other" as an evil enemy it is easy to become closed off to any possibility of addressing communal anxiety through dialogue, reason or negotiation.[8] Rather, responses to communal anxiety becomes a "zero sum game" in which a nation or society will fight to the death to defend what it perceives as right in the face of evil. In other words, when faced with an evil enemy that has been generated as much by social hysteria as actual fact, a self-fulfilling prophecy is created. A nation must act, violently if necessary, to preserve what is good and right and just. It must act for self-preservation. This is

---

[4] Ibid. 213.
[5] Panikos Panayi, *The Enemy in our Midst: Germans in Britain during the First World War* (New York: Berg, 1991), 74. A similar study is Russell A. Kazal, *Becoming Old Stock: The Paradox of German-American Identity* (Princeton, NJ: Princeton University Press, 2004). Russell's study reviews the status of German-American cultural associations during and after World War I.
[6] Panayi, 156.
[7] Ibid., 157-158.
[8] Cole, 232.

the insidious human drive to construct an identity for the nameless, faceless "Other" that provides an easy remedy to the difficult dilemmas of national, economic, and geo-political uncertainties. Is the person sitting on the next bench a witch, a vampire, a German spy, or a terrorist? How can anyone in society be safe with the "Other" in its midst? The easiest response to these anxieties is to let the fear drive the community to develop an identity of the "Other," even if that identity has no relationship to the actual person. What would it take in anxious moments for the German neighbor to cease being a neighbor, and to suddenly become a "spy" or a "terrorist"?

This is not to detract from the veracity that there may be practical and very real national, economic or social ills and dangers plaguing a society. But the drive to solve these crises and return society to balance, equilibrium, justice and equity can be so powerful as to override the moral considerations. An anxious society can point to the necessity of teleological ethics to justify violent means. In such a context it becomes very easy to disrupt the possibility of even seeing the "Other" for who they really are. Rather, a villain is constructed in order to create balance and order. An evil community will represent the antagonist to one's own national or communal myths. For example, Muhammad Abd al-Salam al-Faraj, the leader of the 1970's Egyptian organization *al-Jihad*, created the identity of Pharaoh in President Anwar Sadat.[9] It was Pharaoh and his followers who oppressed the true believers. Thus, to eradicate Pharaoh and his cohort was to return Egyptian society to its true Muslim equilibrium. For Osama Bin Laden, the "Zionist-Crusaders" are the enemy who have besieged the Muslim faithful continually from the fall of Jerusalem in 1099 to the present invasion of Iraq in 2003.[10]

---

[9] Jamal al-Banna and Muhammad `Abd al-Salam Faraj, *al-Farīdah al-ghaibah* (Cairo: Dar Thabit, 1984).

[10] For selections of Bin Laden's messages see Bruce Lawrence, *Messages to the World: The Statements of Osama Bin Laden* (London: Verso, 2005), 32-43.

The nameless, faceless *Jihadist*[11]

The Park 51 or "Ground Zero Mosque" dispute in New York City in 2010 is a contemporary manifestation of Cole and Panayi's observations. The vitriolic public response to the proposition by a leading American Muslim of inter-religious dialogue is an example of choosing to create and construct our own image of the "Other." The media castigation of Imam Faisul Rauf as a Radical Islamist masquerading as a peace-loving Liberal created a mass hysteria, not of German "spy fever," but of *Jihadists* planting the Islamic flag over the ashes of Ground Zero. Such a public atmosphere created a "zero sum" alternative where it was either the triumph of al-Qaeda, or the destruction of the American way of life.

The vehement and venomous response to the Park 51 proposal has rested on a number of assumptions: 1) that Islam is by its very nature violent, 2) that Muslims as a group support the *jihad* against the infidel US, and 3) that Islam is inherently un-American and stands against the freedoms of America. Here we see Samuel Huntington's Clash of Civilization thesis brought into the light of day through public action. In the words of Bernard Lewis, a proponent of this Clash thesis;

> This is no less than a clash of civilizations—the perhaps irrational but surely historic reaction of an ancient rival against our Judeo-Christian heritage, our secular present, and the worldwide importance of both.[12]

Of course, this thesis feeds assumptions, nourishes national anxieties, and creates an image of the Muslim in America. Imam Rauf can be nothing other than another Faisal Shahzad, the New York City bomber. Muslims can be nothing other than joyful at the sight of the falling twin towers. Islam cannot rest until it has conquered. In saner moments perhaps a

---

[11] I am using the term "jihadist" as the anglicized form of one engaging in violent "jihad," as opposed to "Islamist" or "Fundamentalist." See Martin Kramer, "Coming to Terms: Fundamentalists or Islamists?" *Middle East Quarterly* (Spring 2003): 65-77. For further information on the debate of the nomenclature of violent Muslim agendas see Richard Booney, *Jihād: From Qur'ān to bin Laden* (New York: Palgrave Macmillan, 2004); Khaled Abou el Fadl *The Great Theft: Wrestling Islam from the Extremists* (San Francisco: Harper Collins, 2005); and William B. Shepherd, "The Diversity of Islamic Thought: Towards a Typology," in *Islamic Thought in the Twentieth Century*, eds. Suha Taji-Farouki and Basheer M. Nafi (Londn: I.B. Tauris, 2009): 61-103.

[12] Bernard Lewis, "The Roots of Muslim Rage," *Atlantic Monthly* (September 1990), 60.

society can dispute such assumptions, but in anxious national moments, will it?

The above assumptions seek not to address the very complex reality of inter-faith, inter-cultural, inter-national, global economic issues, but rather provide an enemy to redress the imbalance of our own national myths. As Emran Qureshi and Michael A. Sells have written:

> That such a clash is not the product of particular historical circumstances that can change but that the essence of Islam as a religion is antipathetic to the fundamental core values of the West; that Islam is inherently violent in nature; and that, therefore violent attacks against the West are inevitable and are provoked not by any particular grievances or set of circumstances but by the very existence of Western civilization.[13]

To assert, as Qureshi and Sells do, that our current geo-political context and security situation may be the result of "historical circumstances" is too complicated, too intricate, too complex to either understand or to attempt to solve for society at large. Propaganda based upon global inequalities, cultural and linguistic barriers, and economic disequilibrium does not sell. Rather, it is easier to provide answers and restore normalcy by creating the nameless, faceless *Jihadist* who might be sitting on the bus next to us. Rid ourselves of that *Jihadist* and we rid ourselves of our problem and our anxiety. But then, of course, we may still not have solved our problems that have plagued us in the first place. We may not have addressed the problems of these "historical circumstances." And, in the process we may have gotten rid of Ahmed the doctor, whose life has been in pursuit of saving life, not taking it. If it is not an essentialist Islam that is the problem for Americans, but "historical circumstances" in which Muslims find themselves for which they share responsibility, then perhaps the answers to violence may be a bit more complicated than some have imagined.

Fethullah Gülen's critique of violence in the name of Islam[14]

One particular face of Islam that has been outspoken against violence is Fethullah Gülen. In an interview given in 2004 Gülen publicly stated

---

[13] Emran Qureshi and Michael Anthony Sells, eds, *The New Crusades: Constructing the Muslim Enemy* (New York: Columbia University Press, 2003), 2.

[14] Fethullah Gülen, "In True Islam, Terror Does Not Exist," in Ergün Capan, ed., *Terror and Suicide Attacks: An Islamic Perspective* (New Jersey: Light, 2005), 1-8.

> In Islam, killing a human is an act that is equal in gravity to unbelief. No person can kill a human being. No one can touch an innocent person, even in time of war. No one can give a *fatwa* . . .in this matter. No one can be a suicide bomber. No one can rush into crowds with bombs tied to his or her body. Regardless of the religion of these crowds, this is not religiously permissible. Even in the event of war—during which it is difficult to maintain balances—this is not permitted in Islam.[15]

Gülen is clear. Violence perpetrated upon innocents may originate for any number of reasons, but it is not religiously permissible. It is not Islamic. In fact, contrary to those *jihadists* that have declared *takfīr* [or unbelief] on those Muslims who have aided and abetted the West, Gülen argues that those who undertake violence in the name of Islam cannot even be true Muslims. Here is a Muslim voice articulating a message different than that of the *jihadists*.[16] The question is, will this voice be recognized by a society seeking to confront its own anxieties?

What is significant about Gülen's response is that while it might be convenient to fall into the trap of blaming an inherent Clash of Civilizations that gives rise to religiously motivated violence, he looks inward. Communal anxiety should not be placed upon another; rather Gülen questions the historical circumstances that have given rise to this movement of violence in the first place:

> … what efforts did *we* make to raise these people as perfect humans? With what kind of elements did *we* bind them? What kind of responsibility did *we* take in their upbringing so that now *we* should expect them not to engage in terror?[17]

Gülen's critique of the violent *jihadist's* response and search for answers is not surprising. Given the Gülen movement's focus on reading circles which provide social networks for the purpose of spiritual and educational development, the onus is focused inward, not toward a nameless, faceless

---

[15] Capan,1.
[16] See also Steven Wright, "The Work of Fethullah Gülen and the Role of Non-Violence in a Time of Terror," *Fethullah Gülen: Understanding and Respect*, accessed October 30, 2010, http://en.fgulen.com/conference-papers/contributions-of-the-Gülen-movement/302-contributions-of-the-Gülen-movement/2461-the-work-of-fethullah-Gülen-and-the-role-of-non-violence-in-a-time-of-terror.html.
[17] Capan, 5. My emphasis.

"Other."[18] This is a positive and constructive voice that seeks to provide the "Other" with a name, a face and a history.

Rather than seeking to find balance in national communal myths, by looking outward, Christians and Muslims must take seriously what each faith professes about the human-divine relationship. As humans we are either created in the "image of God" (Gen. 1:26-27) or as the graciously created *khalifah* (2:30). Genesis 1:26-27 recalls the important theological narrative for the creation of humanity:

> Then God said, "Let us make humankind in our image, according to our likeness . . . So God created humankind in his image, in the image of God he created them; male and female he created them.

According to the social statement of the Evangelical Lutheran Church in America, "For Peace in God's World:"

> God created all things and gives unity, order, and purpose to a world of different creatures. All humans are created in the image of God (Genesis 1:27), made for life in community—with God, with others, and with the rest of creation.[19]

Humanity, then, has a special relationship with God apart from other creatures in that it is somehow in his image, or by his Will. Thus, *all* of humanity inherits a unique standing within creation, as opposed to one particular nation or family. While the Biblical narrative and the Qur'anic text follow the story of particular families within creation, it is the original divine intention to endow and draw all of Humankind within its fold. Humanity shares a "common foundation upon which to construct an ethical language that can be shared cross-culturally" and dare we say cross-faithfully.[20] This is not only wishful thinking but also a divine intention. Surah *Baqarah* reflects this intended role of humanity within the created order.

---

[18] See "Dying for a Cause: Youth, Violence, and the Gülen Movement—Beyond Tolerance and Dialogue," Georgetown University Conference on "The Gülen Movement," November 14, 2008, accessed October 25, 2010,
http://en.fgulen.com/conference-papers/Gülen-conference-in-washington-dc/3113-dying-for-a-cause-youth-violence-and-the-Gülen-movementbeyond-tolerance-and-dialogue.html.
[19] "For Peace in God's World," ELCA Social Statement, 1995, accessed October 25, 2010, http://archive.elca.org/socialstatements/peace/default.asp.
[20] Abdulaziz Sachedina, "Human Viceregency: A Blessing or a Curse?" in *Humanity Before God,* eds. William Schweiker, Michael A. Johnson, and Kevin Jung, eds., (Minneapolis: Augsburg Fortress, 2006), 43.

> When your Lord said to the angels: 'I am placing on the earth one that shall rule as My deputy [*khalifah*]," they replied: 'Will You put there one that will do evil and shed blood, when we have for so long sung Your praises and sanctified Your name?' He said: 'I know what you know not" (2:30; Dawood).

Each human is endowed with the potential and the responsibility for undertaking God's path in the world, and for reflecting God's intentions for the earth. Thus, within each Scripture and faith tradition humanity has a responsibility toward the creation, including its own species. Beginning with such a starting point, individuals and societies might choose to undertake more virtuous acts on behalf of all Humanity.

> We have ordained a law and assigned a path for each of you. Had God pleased, He could have made of you one community; but it is His wish to prove you by that which He has bestowed upon you. Vie with each other in good works, for to God shall you all return and He will resolve your differences for you (5:48, Dawood).

By viewing the "Other" as sharing a common humanity, with a name and a face, communities might be less prone to construct the "Other" to reduce its own anxieties. Rather, by allowing them to speak for themselves and define themselves and their circumstances, this then would begin the process to "unbind" them from the particular "elements" that engender their choices to engage in terror, as Gülen says.

Conclusion

In times of communal anxiety, in order to seek balance and stability within the national experience, racial, ethnic or religions minorities can be be viewed as less than human; as something other than a creature of the Creator. The "Other" is demonized and their humanness is disrupted from our view so that the nation or community can condemn, act, and validate its own existence. Otherwise, to willingly act violently against one of God's own beloved creatures, God's very own Vice Regent or Creature would create psychological and spiritual trauma upon the conscience of the believer. Fethullah Gülen has been an outspoken critic of the use of violence in the name of Islam. He has been a Muslim voice for peace and inter-faith dialogue. Muslims like Gülen, and Rauf, and Ahmed, and the nameless *muhajibāt* do have a Muslim voice and a Muslim face. The question is, can this face of Islam be recognized?

JUSTICE AND CHARITY: CONTRASTING AND COMPLEMENTARY APPROACHES TO CREATING THE IDEAL SOCIETY

JOSEPH STOUTZENBERGER

In *Love and Tolerance*, Fethullah Gülen speaks of the need to work towards creating an ideal society. Justice is a key component of such a society as Gülen envisions it. However, justice is not only a goal but a means to the goal. Justice implies an approach to addressing what Gülen calls the "nightmare scenario" of injustices such as "the fact that at the present time half the world is living on two dollars a day, with a billion people surviving on even less."[1] When we hear reports such as this, an immediate response may be to provide charity if we can to help people who are suffering. But is charity the answer? Is charity a means to justice, or is justice a different approach to addressing how people are hurting in the world? Are there scenarios in which charity is appropriate and other scenarios in which it is actually detrimental to making life better for people?

In this chapter I will contrast a charity versus a justice approach to helping people in need and to transforming society. I will use two Nobel Peace Prize winners, Mother Teresa and Muhammad Yunus, to illustrate key differences between the two approaches. I will suggest questions to ask as we go about the task set before us by Fethullah Gülen of seeking to overcome injustices and to create an ideal society.

People concerned about social problems typically call for "justice." However, in popular usage the term lacks precision. If we are to get beyond the word as a vague rallying call to make the world a better place for humans and nonhumans alike, then there needs to be some elementary discussion of what justice means. Sometimes the term refers to a goal such

---

[1] Fethullah Gülen, *Toward a Global Civilization of Love and Tolerance* (Somerset, NJ: The Light, 2004), 236.

as a society in which the basic needs of all people are met and all people have equal access to the goods of society—traditionally called distributive justice. Justice can also refer to a particular approach to addressing problems within a society—what might be called a social-justice approach. I would like to identify characteristics of this second understanding of justice by contrasting it with another approach to addressing problems, charity. I find that my own students typically view "charity" as a concrete, caring, and tangible response to helping people who are hurting while justice is seen as an abstract, impersonal notion that does not provide any of the immediate help that people in trouble are crying out for. My sense is that this preference for charity over justice extends beyond my classroom to the larger world community. Magazines display photos of starving children holding out their empty bowls with a plea to send food to feed them. Talk-show host Glenn Beck considers social justice to be not merely ineffective but downright subversive. Early in 2010 he called upon Christians to "leave their social justice churches." He and many others apparently see social justice and socialism as synonymous, while in his mind Americans have always been known for and should continue to practice the nobler endeavor—charity. In this chapter I will describe major differences between these two approaches. I will lay out an explanation of what social justice means in order to identify ways that this approach can be applied to Fethullah Gülen's vision of what he calls an ideal society, especially as it relates to eco-justice.

* * *

In his 2004 book *Toward a Global Civilization of Love and Tolerance*, Fethullah Gülen provides a meditation on "people of heart." Such people "think of mercy, speak of mercy, and seek ways to express themselves through mercy….they believe that being with the oppressed is the same as being with God, and thus support them."[2] Later in the same book he speaks about "an ideal society" that can be brought about through "ideal people" who "courageously devote themselves to ridding the world of injustice and tyranny…they examine all that occurs like a scientist in a laboratory…they dedicate their lives to humanity and leave a much better world for coming generations."[3] Gülen asks: "How many people can we name who try to examine their own beings…trying to study themselves realistically in order to diagnose the disease?"[4] He is brutally honest about

---

[2] Ibid., 23.
[3] Ibid., 129-30.
[4] Ibid., 234-35.

what he calls the "nightmare scenario" that is our world without the values of people of heart. He catalogues hurtful conditions that must be addressed if we are to transform the world in positive ways:

> The fact that at the present time half the world is living on two dollars a day, with a billion people surviving on even less, the fact that a quarter of the world does not have access to healthy drinking water, that the most terrible of diseases, like AIDS, have a tendency to spread rapidly and thus threaten humanity, the fact that health, which is the most vital need of humanity, has become an industry with very expensive services, the fact that global warming and pollution is rife, the fact that a major proportion of the world's population is living without any democratic rights, the fact that human rights violations have become the norm, that living conditions in many places of the world are abysmal, and that unpreventable acts of national and international terrorism reign will be the fearful reality for the whole of humanity.[5]

Clearly Gülen understands the problems we face as a world community. In fact, his list of hurtful conditions mirrors the conditions that the United Nations is currently asking the world community to address in its Millenium Development Goals set for 2015. There are so many ways that people are suffering. A question we need to include in a discussion about such problems is: What are the best ways to address them, alleviate them, and prevent them from recurring? In the world community, are certain methods given priority while others are overlooked? Here's a story that illustrates two approaches to helping people, and we might add helping our environment in need.

> Once upon a time there was a small village on the edge of a river. The people there were good, and life in the village was good. Then one day a villager noticed a baby floating down the river. She quickly jumped into the water and swam out to save the baby from drowning.

> The next day this same villager was walking along the river bank and noticed two babies in the river. She called for help, and both babies were rescued from the currents. The following day four babies were seen caught in the turbulent waters. And then eight, then more, and still more.

> The villagers organized themselves quickly, setting up watch towers and training teams of swimmers who could resist the swift waters and rescue babies. Rescue squads were soon working twenty-four hours a day. But each day the number of babies floating down the river increased.

---

[5] Ibid., 236-37.

The villagers organized themselves efficiently. Rescue squads were now snatching many children each day out of the water. Groups were trained to give CPR. Others prepared formula and provided clothing for the chilled babies. Many people were involved in making clothing and knitting blankets. Still others provided foster homes.

While not all the babies were saved, the villagers worked tirelessly and felt they were doing well to save as many as they did. One day, however, a villager raised the question: "But where are all these babies coming from? How are they ending up in the river? Why? Let's organize a team to go upstream and discover the source of the problem." The elders of the village countered: "But if we go upstream, who will operate the rescue operations? We need every concerned person here."

"But don't you see," cried one lone voice, "if we find out why they are in the river in the first place, then we might be able to stop the problem and no babies will drown. By going upstream, we could eliminate the cause of the problem."

"Our job is saving babies," decided the elders, "not expeditions upstream. We must continue our good work."

And so the number of babies in the river increases daily. Those saved increase, but those who drown increase even more.[6]

This gruesome account of drowning babies is symbolic of Gülen's nightmare scenario. In our world today babies are literally drowning. In parts of the world people are living in shacks over open sewers, and on occasion babies do slip into the polluted waters and are washed away. In other parts of the world babies and other vulnerable people are drowning in poverty and unhealthy living conditions. If we see a child drowning, we want to rescue it. But should Gülen's people of heart be people who also go upriver? What exactly does it mean to "go upriver"? Are rescuing babies in the river and going upstream complementary or opposing approaches to a problem?

The story implicitly contrasts what we might call works of mercy or charity with works of justice. Here are four differences between a charity and a justice approach to social problems implied in the story:

Charity concerns itself with current symptoms of a problem while justice looks for underlying causes of a problem and works to alleviate

---

[6] Adapted from Inter-Religious Task Force for Social Analysis, *Must We Choose Sides?* (1979), 114-15. Also found in Joseph Stoutzenberger, *Justice and Peace* (Dubuque, IA: Brown-ROA, 2000), 68.

those causes. Since our focus is on eco-justice, here's an example of what going upriver means in relation to an environmental concern. In July 2010 *Health* magazine reported on a study published in the *American Journal of Psychiatry* that found that suicide rates in South Korea increased among people with asthma during periods of increased air pollution.[7] While the study doesn't conclusively prove that air pollution makes asthma worse—which in turn affects brain functioning, it is this type of probing that eco-justice calls for. We can pour our resources into better medical care for people with asthma, but if we're serious about addressing the problem, there are underlying causes—environmental causes—that also need to be addressed.

Secondly, charity looks for immediate, temporary solutions while justice looks for long-term solutions. In 2002 the African nation of Zambia faced a dilemma that pitted immediate aid against long-term consequences. Despite widespread hunger problems, the Zambian government refused to accept genetically modified corn from other countries. The fear was that planting such corn hurt small farmers and required large-scale and environmentally harmful farming techniques. The Jesuit Center for Theological Reflection in Zambia supported the government in its decision. This past April Father Peter Henriot from the center said that, "justice in Africa demands a commitment to a long-term sustainability that is impossible with short term environmental damage."[8] Long-term negative consequences often result from food aid given to poor countries. If local markets are inundated with free or inexpensive grain, small local farmers can't compete. Large farmers in wealthy countries receive government subsidies for their contributions of wheat and corn and thus thrive; poor countries and their populations become dependent on foreign aid or charity since they can't sustain themselves.

Thirdly, charity provides direct help to individuals bringing immediate and temporary relief to a limited number of people while justice examines social structures with the intent of bringing about permanent change so that fewer people are in need of charity in the first place. We are all familiar with the phrase: Give people a fish, you feed them for a day; teach people to fish, you feed them for a lifetime. Justice probes even deeper than that, engaging in what we would call "social analysis."[9] Justice

---

[7] See Health.com, "Air Pollution, Asthma Linked to Suicide," July 10, 2010 at http://news.health.com/2010/07/15/air-pollution-asthma-suicide/
[8] "Africa and Justice: Justice in and for Africa," (presented at the Africa Faith and Justice Network Conference, Washington, DC, 17 April, 2010).
[9] See Joe Holland and Peter Henriot, *Social Analysis: Linking Faith and Justice* (Maryknoll, NY: Orbis Books, 1983).

examines how a society's institutions operate in order to bring about institutional changes that benefit all people, especially those people who lack access to benefits and privileges under current arrangements. Thus, rather than giving people fish or even teaching them how to fish, justice asks: Who owns the lake where the fish are? Do some people have access to the lake while others do not? Do only a select group of people have the capital and the connections to get the supplies necessary for profitable fishing? Are workers all along the chain of packaging, transporting, and selling fish paid fairly? We could go on listing questions that would help us examine how social structures foster justice or injustice and unfairly distribute benefits and burdens within a society.

Globalization is a development that demands analysis in terms of who benefits and who suffers because of the way the global market system operates. For instance, most Americans don't care to pay an extra few dollars for a pound of fair-trade coffee or go to the trouble to determine whether gender equity is practiced in development projects. The pressure on poorer people and poor countries is even greater to accept or buy, usually with borrowed money, cheaper goods that in the long run will push them deeper into poverty. "Fair Trade Certified" declares that family farmers receive a fair price for their products that are produced using environmentally sustainable conditions and fair labor practices. [10] Fair trade, not aid, is justice applied to the system of production and distribution of goods so that people most in need can maintain a sustainable living standard long term.

Finally, charity means that "haves" in a society give to "have nots." On the other hand, justice seeks to transform society so that "have nots" have the power to participate actively in society along with the "haves." That is, justice is about empowerment. Justice concerns itself not only with whether or not people's physical needs are met but also with their sense of security, personal dignity, and power. Systems of dominance and oppression create mindsets that make the status quo appear to be unchangeable. Here's an example of empowering a formerly powerless group from the Catholic tradition. In 1891 Pope Leo XIII issued the encyclical *Rerum novarum*, "On the Condition of Labor." This letter from the pope is recognized as the beginning of modern Catholic social teaching. In it the pope calls upon factory owners to treat their workers fairly, which an advocate of charity would certainly agree with. However, the pope goes one step further and declares that workers have a right to form "free

---

[10] See for instance, "Ground for Changes" website for more on Fair Trade Certification: http://www.groundsforchange.com/

associations"—that is, to join unions as a base of power to offset the unbridled power of owners. This tenet in the encyclical upset many people within the European establishment of the time. It was declaring that workers need not depend on charity and the good will of owners alone but have a right to assert their own power. The American priest Fr. John Ryan, who did the most to promulgate Catholic social teaching in America following *Rerum novarum*, wrote that: "Charity is a poison when taken as a substitute for justice."[11] The 1891 papal encyclical, therefore, represents the beginnings of modern Catholic social teaching because it began discussion of social problems from a new perspective, that of social justice. The principle of human beings "working with" the rest of nature, respecting the inherent dignity of all creation, is an important component of eco-justice as well. However, the "haves" of the world suffer the least from environmental degradation even though they consume a disproportionate amount of the earth's resources. "Have nots" must deal most directly with human mistreatment of the rest of nature, and unfortunately, concern for natural resources gets overlooked when people are desperately poor and struggling merely to survive.

* * *

Two Nobel Peace Prize recipients illustrate the difference between charity and justice. The Catholic nun Mother Teresa, awarded the Peace Prize in 1979, was teaching in a girl's school in Calcutta in the late 1940s when she experienced what she termed "a call within a call." She was struck by the many people living in abject poverty in the city. She was particularly moved by the people dying on the streets without anyone to care for them in their final moments of life. She opened a home for the dying and began an order of sisters to take in those people she called "the poorest of the poor." Her approach was essentially to bring them comfort and to let them know that they were loved and cared for as they were dying. She didn't raise questions about why so many people in Calcutta at the time were hungry and homeless and without proper medical care. Later she said that other people may be called to deal with institutions and to change societal structures. Her call was to help individuals, to love each poor person.

Some years ago I heard a lecture in which the speaker praised Mother Teresa for an action she took when she was about to address a conference in London on world hunger. On her way to the convention hall Mother

---

[11] Marvin L. Krier Mich, *Catholic Social Teaching and Movements*, (Mystic, CT: Twenty-Third Publications, 1998), 50.

Teresa came upon a man begging for food. Mother Teresa took the man to a restaurant and bought him a meal, while the people at the conference waited for her to arrive. The speaker applauded Mother Teresa as a person of action who directly helped an actual person who was hungry while the people at the conference were just engaged in talk, not action. In his mind, Mother Teresa's charitable act was a concrete step toward eliminating the real hunger of a real person; justice on the other hand with its focus on systems and long-term goals overlooks the real and immediate needs of actual people.

A more recent Peace Prize recipient is Muhammad Yunus of Bangladesh. In 2006 he received the award along with the bank he founded, Grameen Bank. Yunus is a pioneer in a subset of the social entrepreneurship movement known as micro-finance or social business. A professor of economics, in 1976 Yunus realized that banks were not serving the very people who could benefit most from bank loans—that is, poor people who could not produce any collateral and did not qualify for loans under existing banking systems. When Mother Teresa came upon someone who was hurting, her response was to bring that person to a shelter so that he could die with dignity. Here's how Yunus describes his encounter with a woman named Sufiya who was hurting:

> It seemed to me the existing economic system made it absolutely certain that Sufiya's income would be kept perpetually at such a low level that she would never save a penny and would never invest in expanding her economic base. Her children were condemned to live a life of penury, of hand-to-mouth survival, just as she had lived it before them, and as her parents did before her. I had never heard of anyone suffering for the lack of *twenty-two cents*. It seemed impossible to me, preposterous. Should I reach into my pocket and hand Sufiya the pittance she needed for capital? That would be so simple, so easy. I resisted the urge to give Sufiya the money she needed. She was not asking for charity. And giving one person twenty-two cents was not addressing the problem on any permanent basis.[12]

Yunus began by giving small loans out of his own pocket to a group of women engaged in making bamboo furniture. With the help of the loan the women turned a small profit from their business, and they all repaid the money they were lent. Yunus eventually convinced a Bangladesh bank to work with him in providing small loans to people who were poor but had prospects for ways of making a living. In 1983 he opened his own bank,

---

[12] Muhammad Yunus, *Banker to the Poor: Micro-Lending and the Battle against World Poverty*, (New York: Public Affairs, 2007), 48.

called Grameen (village) Bank. The Grameen Bank micro-finance program has put Bangladesh on track to exceed its timetable for overcoming poverty in the country, and the model has been imitated in other parts of the world that have also been mired in poverty.

Yunus sees the shortcomings to charity that I mentioned earlier. He writes: "Charity...has a significant built-in weakness. It relies on a steady stream of donations by generous individuals, organizations, or government agencies. When these funds fall short, the good works stop." [13] His approach leads to self-sufficiency among people who would otherwise be stuck in a system of dependency. Yunus' social-business model represents a change in the banking *system*. It empowers previously unempowered people, and it requires "haves" and "have nots" working together. In other words, it is a work of justice. Yunus explains:

> If the poor are to get the chance to lift themselves out of poverty, it's up to us to remove the institutional barriers we've created around them. We must remove the absurd rules and laws we have made that treat the poor as nonentities. And we must come up with new ways to recognize a person by his or her own worth, not by artificial measuring sticks imposed by a biased system. [14]

Clearly there are times when charity is called for. When a relative or neighbor loses her job, it would be heartless not to help out if we can. However, we would be shortsighted if we also didn't look to see what societal values and social structures lead to unemployment and what systemic changes might prevent losing a job from being as devastating as it can be.

Where does Fethullah Gülen fit into this discussion about contrasting approaches to addressing social problems? Gülen doesn't advocate one approach over the other. I would describe his message as beyond these classifications and as providing a litmus test by which to analyze all of our approaches to problems. His concern is primarily what I'd call spiritual. He calls for personal conversion from which people give themselves in service to others. As I mentioned at the beginning, he wants people to "study themselves" and to "examine their own beings." They are to commit themselves to a life of altruism. Only as a result of this personal spiritual transformation will they dedicate themselves to working with others in reconstructing the world through whatever means prove to be effective. He also clearly values science and the scientific method. As a

---

[13] Muhammad Yunus, *Creating a World Without Poverty: Social Business and the Future of Capitalism* (New York: Public Affairs, 2007), 10.

[14] Ibid., 49.

scientist works meticulously in a laboratory, so we are to examine ourselves and the world around us—personal as well as social analysis if you will. The Gülen movement places a high value on education as a means to develop thoughtful, compassionate people. Gülen's emphasis on scientific methods, education, and ongoing self and societal examination belies merely doing works of charity. It sounds a lot like a call to be "upriver" explorers as described in the story beginning this chapter. I'll let Gülen have the last word on the matter:

> I believe with my whole heart that the only thing to do today in order to realize these spring-fragranced dreams is to perform this kind of service for humanity. For this reason, instead of temporary, fleeting, and unpromising efforts, I would advise a type of movement that is lasting and fully beneficial in every way.[15]

---

[15] Gülen, *Love and Tolerance*, 253.

END TIMES FOR THESE TIMES: ESCHATOLOGY-RETURN AND DIALOGUE FOR PEACE

WALTER H. WAGNER

The article seeks to show two points essential to the role of Muhammed Fethullah Gülen and the Hizmet Movement in peace-making with reference to eco-justice, and future inter-religious and inter-ideological dialogues and actions. First, eschatology must have a prominent position in such dialogues and resulting endeavors. Second, Fethullah Gülen's eschatology is determinative in his thinking and influence on and beyond Hizmet (Service).

The article's four sections and conclusion open with a cluster of three relevant terms, ideas and figures. The second portion deals with positions developed by Said Nursi (1876-1960) applicable to Gülen's perspectives.[1] Gülen's views are developed in the third portion. The brief fourth section indicates that Gülen and Hizmet may engage the contributions of two Christian theologians, the Roman Catholic, Hans Küng, and the pentecostal, Amos Yong.[2] The Conclusion is a summary and suggests some directions for future efforts.

Section One: Clusters of Three Key Terms, Ideas and Figures

Future studies of End Times and Hereafters in Judaism, Christianity and Islam for dialogical purposes may expand on the number and uses of terms

---

[1] Because Nursi and Gülen are Sunni Muslims, I forego comparing Shi'ia positions with them. For Shi'ia views, see Mahdi Muntazir Qaim, *Jesus through the Qur'an and Shi`ite Narrations* (New York: Tahrike Tarsile Qur'an, 2005), 234-246 and Muhammad Baqir As-Sadr, *An Inquiry Concerning Al-Mahd.* (Qum, Iran: Ansaryian Publications, n.d.).

[2] The lower case in "pentecostal" indicates a charismatic movement that includes church bodies that use upper case "Pentecostal" in their self-designations.

beyond the present paper. A vital point for our study is that Christianity and Islam share important analogues regarding eschatological expectations, figures, and timings. To be sure, Islam and Christianity include motifs from Judaism. The following are relevant to our study.

1. Eschatology

Eschatology is a neglected subject in inter-religious dialogues. Yet End Time emphases involve preparing for the future through seeking to establish justice, peace and love in the present. Eschatology provides a proleptic dynamic that pushes present persons and proposals toward the future and an analeptic perspective through which the future is anticipated in the present. While prophets and seers attempt to describe sights that loom in the future, they and their eschatological pronouncements deeply engage affairs in the present. Considerations of the End Times are simultaneously cosmic in scope, communal in nature and individual in application. Tim Winter indicated the range of eschatological concerns:

> Eschatology embraces not only teachings about death, resurrection, immortality and judgment, but also the tradition's understanding of beginnings, the meaning of history and the direction and purpose towards which everything in creation tends. [3]

Eschatology embraces three aspects. First, *eschaton* connotes last, uttermost and final. Second, the concept involves *telos*, that is, goal, completion and fulfillment. Third, eschatology is grounded in the claims and problems of theodicy; how and why God directs the course of events and futures for individuals, communities and the universe. Christian and Muslim eschatologies hold that God has a plan for time, the cosmos and creatures.[4] Nature, events and people are moving toward their divinely determined eschaton-telos. In that light, Islam and Christianity are profoundly eschatological. Ethics within those faith communities, between them, and toward the world are more than matters of prudence; they aim at the end as finality and fullness. Eschatological works and portions thereof regularly call on the members of their communities to be patient, loyal, and morally pure as the cosmic drama unfolds around and through them. Eschatological-Apocalyptics often offer final scenes for life in the present world that involve massive divine interventions, savior-rescuers and their

---

[3] Tim Winter, ed., *Classical Islamic Theology* (Cambridge, UK: Cambridge University Press, 2008), 308.

[4] E.g., Ephesians 1:3-14 and Qur'an 3:54, 27:50.

evil counterparts, resurrection of the dead, and judgment usually based on deeds. There are no strict definitions for apocalyptic expressions and literature.[5] The end of this world serves as the opening for newly created worlds that promise humans eternal bliss or threaten them with deserved eternal punishment.

In one sense, most systematic theologians are correct to begin their expositions about God with creation and conclude with reflections on this creation's termination and what may lie beyond it.[6] Nevertheless, one may argue that eschatology deserves to be put first in attempting to understand Islam and Christianity. After all, Jesus, most New Testament writers, Muhammad and the Qur'an placed it at the beginning of their proclamations about God, the world and humanity.[7] Muslim and Christian communities continue to profess, at least formally, the conviction that God will end this world, resurrect the dead, judge all persons and provide everlasting hereafters for them. Both traditional Christianity and Islam look forward to Jesus' return and participation in the End Times.[8] How seriously present-day Christians retain eschatological expectations is debatable. Muslims are consistent in keeping belief in the Return, Resurrection, Day of Judgment and life in the Hereafter as parts of their essential teachings. Muslim thinkers who hold to traditional understandings of the Qur'an's inspiration and authority and the authority of the pure (sahih) Hadith collections

---

[5] Walls Jerry Walls, ed., *The Oxford Handbook of Eschatology* (New York: Oxford University Press, 2008), 3.

[6] E.g., among Christians, see Karl Rahner, *Foundations of the Christian Faith* (New York: Seabury Press, 1978); Francis Fiorenza-Schüssler and John Galvin, eds. *Systematic Theology. Roman Catholic Perspectives*, Vol. 2 (Minneapolis: Fortress Press, 1991); Carl Braaten and Robert Jenson, eds. *Church Dogmatics*, Vol. 2 . (Philadelphia: Fortress Press, 1984); John Macquarrie, *Principles of Christian Theology* (New York: Scribners Sons, 1977); Alister McGrath, *Christian Theology: An Introduction*. 2nd ed., (Oxford: Blackwells, 1997); and Paul Tillich, *Systematic Theology*. Vol. 3, (Chicago: University of Chicago Press, 1963). For Muslims, see Tim Winter, ed., *Classical Islamic Theology* (Cambridge, UK: Cambridge University Press, 2008).

[7] See Mark 1:14-15; Matthew 25, 1 Corinthians 15; the Revelation to John for Christians. See also in the Qur'an passages such as Surahs 96:1-5; 7; 79-86; 88-89. Note: Muslims use the reverential honorifics Peace and Blessings Be Upon Him when referring to God's Messengers. I acknowledge that use at this point and ask readers to assume it for the rest of the paper. The translation of the Qur'an used in the paper is that by Ali Ünal.

[8] E.g., the Nicene-Constantinopolitan Creed, and Muslim citations about Jesus (e.g., Abu'l-Husain Muslim, *Sahih Muslim*, trans. Abdul Hamid Siddiqi, vol. 4, bk 39, ch. 1198 (New Delhi, Kitab Bhavan, 1986), 1, 501.

accept the End Time and Hereafter positions revealed in the Qur'an and expressed in the Hadith while not neglecting allegorical or spiritual interpretations along with the literal texts.[9] Gülen is one of those thinkers.

2. Messiahs-Anti-Messiahs-Guides-Renewers

Eschatological savior-rescuer figures are necessary in traditional Islam and Christianity. Both religions also feature counter-saviors. First, messiah-christ.

A. Messiah-Christ

A messiah-christ is a human or high-ranking angel regarded as anointed and/or empowered by God to fulfill God's will. In the Jewish portions of the early First Century CE work, 2 Esdras, two figures are called "messiah." One is a human from the family of David and the other an angelic being.[10] The human messiah is hidden by God until a God-appointed time. He will emerge to defeat evil, liberate God's elect, head a temporary bountiful and joyful kingdom for four hundred years, then die. Following his death, the world will be returned to its pre-creation "primeval silence" until a new creation is roused into existence by God.[11] The new creation will open with judgment, rewards and punishment. The second messiah is an angelic figure who appears as the "man from the sea" to destroy evil forces, liberate God's people, and make them joyful until the day judgment (13:1-52). In both instances, the final day will be prefaced with a period of joy, prosperity and peace headed by a God-appointed leader.

Although Christians and Muslims consider Jesus-'Isa to be the messiah-christ, they have obviously similar and different functions and expectations for him. Neither Islam nor Christianity agrees fully with 2 Esdras, yet elements in the Esdras tradition are noteworthy. 2 Esdras was included in some printed Bibles as an appendix, while the Qur'an (Surah 9:30) reflects the position of 2 Esdras 14:9 that the scribe was raised to angelic or even higher divine rank. Nevertheless, both religions believe

---

[9] Generally, Muslims scholars "assess the relative validity of hadith texts: *sahih* ("sound", the most acceptable; *hasan* (*good*), somewhat below the first in excellence; and daif (weak"))." See John Esposito, ed., *The Oxford Encyclopedia of the Modern Islamic World*, vol. 2 (New York: Oxford University Press, 1995), 84.
[10] 2 Esdras 7:26-41, 11:36-12:36 and 13:1-52.
[11] The human messiah is not mentioned as among the resurrected dead.

that Jesus-'Isa will be involved in evil's defeat and the establishment of realms of justice and peace.

B. Anti-Messiahs-Anti-Christs

Islam and Christianity have traditions about false or counter-messiahs or antichrists According to the synoptic Gospels, Jesus warned his followers that prior to the Last Days pseudo-christs will appear to deceive many on earth, some claiming to be the returned Jesus.[12] The writer(s) of 1 John and 2 John use the term "antichrist" in the singular and plural. The singular antichrist is yet to come, but there are many antichrists in the present and who defected from the author(s)' congregations. [13] The Revelation/Apocalypse to John features an evil beast who transitions into being a false prophet who deceives many by doing signs and wonders, seals the deluded with the mark of the beast, then organizes the kings to fight God at Har-Megiddo only to be defeated and thrown alive into the lake of burning sulfur.[14] Beginning in the Second Century, the Johannine antichrist and the Revelation false prophet were amalgamated into a demonically empowered human being.[15]

Islam has the *Massih al-Dajjal*, the false or imposter messiah, often translated as Antichrist. His appearance is one of the ten major signs that the Last Day is drawing near.[16] According to a Hadith from Bukhari, "About thirty Dajjal appear, and each one will claim he is Allah's messenger."[17]

---

[12] E.g., Mark 13:21-23 and Luke 21:7-8.

[13] 1 John 2:18-23 refers to a single future *antichristos* and *antichristoi* in the present. 2 John 7 defines anyone who rejects the humanity of Jesus as an antichrist.

[14] Revelation 13:11-18, 16:12-16, 19:17-21.

[15] See Hippolytus, "Treatise on Christ and Antichrist" in Alexander Roberts and James Donaldson, eds., *Ante-Nicene Fathers*, vol. 5 (Grand Rapids: Eerdmans, 1957), 204-221 and Bernard McGinn, *Antichrist. Two Thousand Years of the Human Fascination with Evil* (San Francisco: HarperSan Francisco, 1994). McGinn, Antichrist.

[16] See Muslim, bk. 39, ch. 1202, hadith 6931: the smoke, Dajjal, beast, rising of the sun from the west, descent of Jesus, Gog and Magog, 3 landslides, and fire from Yemen. InMuslim, bk. 39, ch.1, 212, hadith 7040, six signs were cited: the rising of the sun from the west, the smoke, the Dajjal, the beast, death of one of his listeners or "the general turmoil." *Dajjal* connotes to overlay an object with a precious metal and to hide a product's defects from a buyer.

[17] Muhammad ibn Ismaiel Bukhari. *The Translation of the Meanings of Sahih Al-Bukhari*. Nine Volumes, Muhammad Muhsin Khan, trans., bk. 92, ch. 25, hadith 721:2 (Riyadh: Darussalam, 1997).

The ultimate Dajjal is described as a grotesque human of great power chained in a cave in the east. Some time before the cataclysms of the Last Day, he will burst forth to attack and deceive the inhabitants of the world. He will travel throughout the world except for Mecca, Medina and Damascus.[18] He and his armies will slaughter those who resist his claims to be Allah. He will perform deceptive miracles and attack the remnant of the faithful Muslims. He and his forces will besiege the remnant of faithful Muslims in Jerusalem. The Dajjal will be on the verge of victory when Jesus-'Isa will return from his heavenly place, kill the Dajjal near Jerusalem and the Dajjal's forces will be destroyed.[19] Jesus-'Isa will then inaugurate a period of prosperity, joy, true religion (Islam) and peace. At the end of that period, he will die.

Harun Yahya, quoting pure and weak Hadiths described the period when Jesus-'Isa will rule the earth. Muhammad is reported to have said:

> Jesus, peace be upon him, will be a just judge and a just ruler in my ummah (people) . . . He will abandon the collection of zakat; grudge and mutual hatred will be lifted (removed), the sting of every stinging insect will be removed until a baby will insert his finger in snake's mouth and it will not harm him, and the wolf will be like the dog among the sheep (safeguarding them). Earth will be filled with peace, just as a vessel is filled with water; the word (*kalima*) will become one (i.e., only Islam will prevail) and only God will be worshipped; the battle will put down its weapons (i.e., come to an end) and the dominion of the Qurayshis will be broken. (*Sunan Ibn Majah*).
>
> [In his time], there will be no rancour between any two persons. (*Sahih Muslim*). [In his time], peace will prevail and people will use their swords as sickles. Every harmful beast will be made harmless . . . A child will play with a fox and not come to any harm;a wolf will graze with sheep and a lion with cattle, without harming them.[20]

C. Guides and Renewers

Savior-figures other than Jesus-Isa are part of Muslim and Christian eschatology. Among Christians, the emperor Constantine became a model for the Last Roman Emperor. The latter, a figure expected initially by

---

[18] Muslim, bk. 92, ch. 1211, hadith 7028-7033.

[19] Muslim, bk. 39, ch. 1210, hadith 7023. See also Muslim, bk. 39, ch. 1,207, hadith 7015.

[20] Harun Yahya, *The Glad Tidings of the Messiah* (Istanbul: Global Publishing, 2004), 52.

seventh century Syrian-Mesopotamians, was to defeat the Muslims and open a marvelous age of true Christianity, abundance, prosperity, etc.[21]

Muslims have two figures relevant to our study. The first is the Mahdi. The term means both the Guide and the Guided One. The basic belief is that a man from Muhammad's family and who will bear Muhammad's name will be raised up by God in a time of great turbulence (*fitna*). He will destroy evil or join with Jesus-'Isa in defeating evil. Then, a prosperous age will open. The age will deteriorate, and then Dunya (this world) will end, Judgment and the Afterlife (Ahkira) will be revealed. Sunni Mahdism's positions vary. Some stress the Mahdi as the one who will introduce a golden age as a glorious time between a first and second Fitna (turbulence). The latter period will lead to the Last Hour.[22] Abu Dawud holds he will come after twelve caliphs, in a time of turmoil for Muslims and the world, and reign "with equity and justice" for seven or nine years.
[23]

The second tradition is a line of figures, the Renewers (*Mujaddid*). They will be especially important in understanding Nursi and Gülen. Dawud reported Muhammad saying: "Allah will raise for this community at the end of every hundred years the one who will renovate its religion for it."[24] The Renewers are scholars, not political or military figures. They are spiritually oriented educators who influence, correct, and influence the umma, and through the umma the world. In this sense the Mujaddids contrast with Mahdi traditions. Belief in the periodic rise and influences of Renewers may help explain how many Muslims are able to cope with disasters, defeats and divisions without resorting to despair, apostasy or violence. Forms of Mahdism, on the other hand, may trigger actions intended to hasten the apocalyptic signs of the coming golden age.[25]

3. Millennialism

"Millennium" refers to one thousand. Its eschatological expression surfaced in and is unique to the New Testament's Revelation (Apocalypse) to John. Revelation 17-19 recounts the fall of Babylon (Rome, depicted as

---

[21] See McGinn, *Antichrist*, 66-76 and Alexander, 48-50.
[22] See Harun Yahya, *The End Times and the Mahdi* (Istanbul: Khatoons, 2003), 33-58.
[23] Abu Dawud, *Sunan Abu Dawud*, Ahmad Hasan, trans., vol. 3, bk. 31, ch. 1586 (Lahore: Sh. Muhammad Ashraf, 2004 reprint).
[24] Dawud, vol. 3, bk. 32, ch. 1587, hadith 4278. See Winter, 316.
[25] Yaroslav Trofimov, *The Siege of Mecca* (New York: Doubleday, 2007).

a whore) and the defeat of her blasphemous beast-throne. Prior to their defeat by the heavenly warrior, Word of God (19:17-21), the whore, beast, a false prophet and his minions rampaged through the world, persecuting Christians, and afflicting the world. Revelation 20:4-5 deals with the millennium after Satan cast into a pit:

> Then I saw thrones, and those seated on them were given authority to judge. I also saw the souls of those who had been beheaded for their testimony to Jesus and for the word of God. They had not worshiped the beast or its image and had not received its mark on their foreheads or their hands. They came to life and reigned with Christ a thousand years. (The rest of the dead did not come to life until the thousand years were ended.) This is the first resurrection.

The book of Revelation and that passage have prompted disputes among Christians since the Second Century. Many Christians are "a-millennialists," that is, they reject the millennium altogether. Very conservative Christians usually accept it.[26] Two interpretive trends have emerged among Millenialists. "Pre-Millennialists" hold that martyrs will be resurrected to enjoy a millennium of blessing in Jesus' physical presence and rule. Post-Millennialists believe that Jesus will not be physically present but will be spiritually influential with the saints. In either case, following the thousand years, Satan will be released and further struggles will ensue. The faithful Christians besieged in Jerusalem by evil forces will be saved by God's fiery destruction of the demonic armies. Following that victory, the old world will disappear, the dead will be raised and judged. Finally, a new heavens and earth centered on the New Jerusalem will appear. Over time, the term "Millennium" came to be used among Muslims and Christians to mean the interim between one struggle with evil forces and the final battles without reference to the literal thousand years.

Section Two: Aspects from Said Nursi

Reflecting on his own life, Nursi recognized three "Saids." The "Old Said" sought to arrest the Ottoman Empire's decline by restoring Islam's guiding principles for the realm. As a Kurd from eastern Anatolia, he was especially sensitive to ethnic tensions within society. The "New Nursi" did

---

[26] See Charles Ryrie, *Dispensationalism* (Chicago: Moody Press, 2007), 171-174 and Paul Benware, *Understanding the End Times: A Comprehensive Approach* (Chicago: Moody Press, 1995), 77-156.

not depart from his earlier principles but was sobered by the demise of the Ottoman Empire following World War I and the modern Turkish Republic's anti-religious secularism. He was more convinced than previously that a reformed educational system that balanced science and religion was essential for Turkey and the world. The "Newest Nursi" emerged in the post World War II period. He was harassed, imprisoned, restricted to an isolated area before being released shortly before his death. During incarceration and isolation, he turned inward, finding solace in the Qur'an while retaining deep concern for his nation and the world. His writings and influence resulted in the Nur (Light) Movement. Through the Movement, many others were inspired by him. One such figure is Fethullah Gülen. Some Turkish Muslims suggest that Nursi is the Mujaddid of the Twentieth Century.

A key to Nursi's thought is his 1911 Damascus Sermon. He diagnosed the ills of Ottoman Islam as despair, deceit, enmity, disunity, despotism and individualism. These were also the ills of the West. He based his therapy on a renewal of Islamic virtues informed by reason, science and a selective appropriation of Western ways. Specifically he prescribed hope, honesty, love, unity, Islamic dignity, and consultation – that is, sincere cooperation and fellowship. Nursi reflected that the world had hit bottom in terms of moral decline, but was beginning to awaken spiritually as the new century dawned. The time was ripe for a Renewer and for Jesus-'Isa to act. Yet, Nursi warned: "If the jewel of true religion is not present in the shell of the heart, material, moral and spiritual calamities of untold magnitude will break loose over mankind and they will become the most unhappy, the most wretched of animals.[27] Three years later, World War I began and Nursi joined the Ottoman army. The Great War and its aftermath transformed him into the "New Nursi." He witnessed and was part of the carnage of the War and the subsequent Turkish War for Independence. Increasingly he moved toward a spiritual understanding of humanity and of the Qur'an without surrendering the need for the improving the physical side of the world. In the Risale-i Nur collection of his writings, he discloses a Quranic hermeneutic that stressed the allegorical meaning of texts.[28] He concluded that the major signs of the End Times described in the Hadith are, at least partially, present-day spiritual struggles. The Dajjal offers a false paradise through modern civilization's passing fancies, materialism, imperialism and the use of technology to bolster exploitation.

---

[27] Said Nursi, *The Damascus Sermon* (Istanbul: Nur Publishers, 1989), 16.
[28] Said Nursi, *The Rays*. Risale-i Nur Collection, Ray 5 (Istanbul: Sözler Publications, 2006), 97f .

While imprisoned he wrote letters to his followers and answered their questions. In his first letter he stated that his foremost concerns were to prove God's existence and unity; bodily resurrection and the Day of Judgment; validity of the Qur'an; and Muhammad's Prophethood. [29]

He stated that the essence of the universe is love and that genuine human love is a figure for the true love of God. He continued that Islamic civilization rests on five factors:

1. The right which requires justice and balance;
2. Encouraging virtues that spur mutual affection and love;
3. Considering life as mutual help leading to unity and solidarity;
4. Unifying people through a common religion leading to peace and brotherhood and resisting external enemies; and
5. Guiding people to truth through involving scientific truth that elevates persons to moral perfection.

In the first letter and subsequently, Nursi wrote about five levels of human existence.[30]

1. Ordinary persons living in this realm of trial and testing;
2. Realm of Khadr and Elijah in which they are not bound by time, location and human needs;
3. Realm of Jesus-'Isa and Enoch. They have ethereal bodies and live an angelic style of life;
4. Realm of the martyrs; and
5. Realm of the spiritual lives of the dead.

Although Jesus-'Isa was on the celestial level, he influenced the world spiritually. Letter 15 took up the conflict between a dajjal, a member of the Prophet's family and Jesus-'Isa. [31] One form of the Dajjal was a hypocritical leader bent on destroying Islamic Sharia who would be exposed and defeated by a blessed member of the Prophet's family. The second Dajjal-tendency was materialistic atheism. He wrote:

> When this trend of atheism is seen almost at its peak, the true, original religion of Jesus will reappear. That is, it will come down from the heaven of Divine mercy, and the present form of Christianity, purified of its borrowed elements, will unite with the truths of Islam or be transformed into it, and will follow the Qur'an. The true religion will gain great strength from this union and defeat the atheistic trend. Based on the

[29] Said Nursi, *The Letters*. Risale-i Nur Collection (Somerset, NJ, 2007), 3-20.
[30] Ibid., 94-95.
[31] Ibid.

promise of the All-Powerful One, The Prophet ... informed that Jesus would come down toward the end of time. ... Remember that Jesus is in the nearest heaven with his refined corporeal body... During this dramatic episode, Islam will be far stronger due to its union with a purified Christianity and will spread its light to the majority of people.[32]

Nursi's expectation that the awakening would start at the onset of the Twentieth Century was premature. Still, he held out the Islamic remedies for the ills of a physically, morally and spiritually violent world. His emphasis became the imminent union of a purified Christianity led by the spiritually present Jesus-'Isa in union with a renewed Islam. And that provided grounds for opening relationships with Christians through cooperation and dialogue.

Section Three: Fethullah Gülen

Although Nursi and Gülen never met and Gülen was not a formal member of the Nur Movement, he was deeply influenced by Nursi. Gülen retains his Turkish grounding while internationalizing the eschatological dynamic through dialogue and direct actions directed toward and based on love. Eschatological dimensions are laced through his writings. A section on the belief in the resurrection and afterlife extols eternal joy in the Hereafter, while emphasizing the influences such an expectation have for present existence. People may look forward now with anticipation to that life and emulate its peacefulness and blessings.[33] His views of the influence of Jesus-'Isa on events and persons follows Nursi's understanding of Jesus-'Isa's role in preparation for the renewal of the earth, human communities and individual spiritual as well as physical lives. Throughout these aspirations and expectations, Gülen shows that all is being moved forward by God's eschatological plan:

> This life is very important, for it shapes the afterlife. Given this, we should spend it in ways designed to earn eternal life and gain the Giver of Life's approval. This path passes through the inescapable dimension of servanthood to God by means of serving, first of all, our families, relatives and neighbors, then our country and nation, and finally humanity and

---

[32] Ibid., 95-96.
[33] Gülen, *The Essentials of Islamic Faith*, (Somerset: The Light, 2006), 129-162.

creation. This service is our right: conveying it to others is our responsibility.[34]

Gülen's "At the Threshold of a New Millennium," may be paralleled to Nursi's Damascus Sermon.[35] As did Nursi, Gülen emphasizes hope, for humans are created by God as people of hope. As mirrors of God's Beautiful Names and Attributes, humans are responsible for making this earth prosperous and peaceful. The way to such a goal in this age is through religion fused with scientific knowledge and infused with morality and spirituality. The result will be a "New Springtime." The eschatological theme of a millennial period may be discerned. He cited the Quranic motif of the cycles of nature disclosing the goodness, generosity and expectations of God for human service, worship, gratitude and action. In this circulation, "God-given human abilities become aptitudes and talents, sciences blossom like roses, and weave technology in the workbench of time, and humanity gradually approaches its predestined end."[36] The old hostile age will be ended through the New Springtime marked by the new style of education that will gradually produce a "genuinely enlightened people," and this will happen before the "demise" of "our old world." Gülen has an eschatological certainty about the success of the New Millennium based on his faith in God and the Qur'an's promises that all began with and will return to God, for God's plan will be fulfilled:

> Yes, this springtime will rise on the foundations of love, compassion, mercy, dialogue, acceptance of others, mutual respect, justice, and rights. It will be a time in which humanity will discover its real essence. Goodness and kindness, righteousness and virtue will form the basic essence of the world. No matter what happens, the world will come to this track sooner or later. Nobody can prevent this.[37]

"Tolerance" recurs throughout Gülen's works. The Turkish word is *hoşgörü*. Normally it means "seeing the other in a good way." Gülen goes further:

> Tolerance (*hoşgörü*), a term which we sometimes use in place of the words respect, mercy, generosity or forebearance, is the most essential element of moral systems; it is a very important source of spiritual discipline and a celestial virtue. Under the lens of tolerance the merits of

---

[34] Gülen, "Education from Cradle to Grave," in *Essays-Perspectives-Opinions* (Rutherford, NJ: Fountain, 2002), 88.
[35] Ibid., "At the Threshold of a New Millennium," 21-31.
[36] Ibid., 23.
[37] Ibid., 31.

believers extend to infinity; mistakes and faults become insignificant and whither away.... In fact, the treatment of He Who is beyond time and space always passes through the prism of tolerance, and we wait for it to embrace us and all creation.[38]

In a 1995 response what was then called the "New World Order," Gülen wrote,

> Even if this world is not in a process of renewal, and it is clear today that it is not, it definitely is in a process of reconstruction. When the correct time arrives, this reconstruction will certainly be realized. When this happens, instead of having a world that has been shaped with malice and hatred, a surprising world that has taken its form in a climate of love, tolerance and forbearance will appear before us. The collective conscience will gladly welcome and place it in its heart, not neglecting those who have a share in this reformation. These people will leave permanent tracks and, even if they have physically left the world, their tracks will remain for centuries. I believe with my whole heart that the only thing to do today in order to realize these spring-fragranced dreams is to perform this kind of service for humanity. For this reason, instead of temporary, fleeting, and unpromising efforts, I would advise a type of movement that is lasting and fully beneficial in every way.[39]

Perhaps his views about a time of renewal brightened. Soon after 1995 he wrote that since the time of Muhammad, persons have extended the prophetic mission up to the present. He cited specifically al-Arabi, al-Ghazali, Rabbani, Khalid and Nursi. These persons "prepare for the foundation of the rebirth of the prophetic spirit in the years to come.[40] This may be Gülen's way of citing the Mujaddids. Countering Samuel Huntington's assertion of a "clash of civilizations," Gülen held that with God's blessings a breeze of tolerance and dialogue was spreading over the world. The Turkish nation, he anticipated, would be the example to bring people together around basic human values so that, "God willing, humankind will live one more spring before seeing the end of the world."[41]

Inter-religious dialogue is a necessity in the process of achieving the realm of peace in the present that anticipates the blessed Hereafter:

---

[38] Gülen. *Love and Tolerance*, 33-34.
[39] Ibid., 253.
[40] Ibid., 254.
[41] Ibid., 257.

People are talking about peace, contentment, ecology, justice, tolerance, and dialogue. Unfortunately the prevailing materialistic worldview disturbs the balance between humanity and nature and within individuals. This harmony and peace only occurs when the material and spiritual realms are reconciled. Religion reconciles opposites... The natural sciences, which should lead people to God, instead cause widespread unbelief. As this trend is strongest in the West, and because Christianity is the most influenced, Muslim-Christian dialogue is indispensable.

Interfaith dialogue seeks to realize religion's basic oneness and unity, and the universality of belief. Religion embraces all beliefs and races in brotherhood, and exalts love, respect, tolerance, forgiveness, mercy, human rights, peace, brotherhood, and freedom via its Prophets.

Islam has a Prophetic Tradition that Jesus will return during the last days. For Muslims this means that such values as love, peace, brotherhood, forgiveness, altruism, mercy and spiritual purification will have precedence. As Jesus was sent to the Jews and all Jewish Prophets exalted these values, dialogue with Jews must be established, as well as a closer relationship among Islam, Christianity and Judaism. [42]

Gülen's Five Pillars of Dialogue are grounded on his (and Nursi's) axiom that love is the essence of the universe. So the Pillars are based in love and culminate in love. The Pillars are: Tolerance or fellow feeling and acceptance, Forgiveness, Compassion, Altruism and Love.[43]

The old hostile age will be ended through the New Springtime marked by the new education that will gradually produce a "genuinely enlightened people," and this will happen before the "demise" of "our old world." Gülen has an eschatological certainty about the success of the New Millennium based on his faith in God and the Qur'an's promises that all began with and will return to God, for God's plan will be fulfilled:

Yes, this springtime will rise on the foundations of love, compassion, mercy, dialogue, acceptance of others, mutual respect, justice, and rights. It will be a time in which humanity will discover its real essence. Goodness and kindness, righteousness and virtue will form the basic essence of the world. No matter what happens, the world will come to this track sooner or later. Nobody can prevent this. [44]

Eschatological urgency pervades Gülen's thought. Eco-justice is one significant manifestation of Islamic-Quranically centered message that energizes the Hizmet Movement and its engagement in deep peace-making

---

[42] Gülen, *Essays-Perspectives-Opinions*, 21-31.
[43] Ibid., 41-42.
[44] Ibid., 31.

among humans and with the creation. His inclusive view of all humans may often be expressed toward Jews and Christians. His scope, more implicitly than explicitly, includes other religions and those who espouse no religious commitments. He specifically summons Christians, Jews and Muslims to a deepened renewal and realization of their profound unity. He stands clearly in the tradition of Muslim Mujaddid. Whether he will be acknowledged as such, as Muslims say, God knows.

Section Four: Suggestions Concerning Hans Küng and Amos Yong

I can only touch upon the possibilities for Küng's and Yong's views being considered in light of Gülen's positions. Küng's statements about the necessity of dialogue are essential for setting Christians and then all others on the path of dialogue:

> No peace among the nations without peace among the religions
> No peace among the religions without dialogue between religions
> No dialogue between the religions without investigation of the foundations of the religions
> No dialogue among the religions without global ethical standards
> No survival of our globe without a global ethic, a world ethic, supported by both the religious and non-religious.[45]

Küng, however, seems to avoid eschatological considerations as he developed his theological positions. His proposals directed toward Muslims and his advice that they adjust their foundational positions in light of Western approaches probably will not be accepted by most Muslims. Nevertheless, his insights about Islam, communicated to non-Muslims are valuable and useful for non-Muslims in their seeking to understand and then engage in dialogue.

Amos Yong, a biblically conservative Malaysian-born Chinese, Assemblies of God theologian, applies his emphasis on the Christian belief in the Holy Spirit of God being poured out on all creation and humans.[46] His global concerns engage persons of many faiths and cultures in understanding the hospitality-openness-acceptance of one another through

---

[45] Hans Küng, *Islam: Past, Present and Future* (Oxford: Oneworld, 2007), 661-662.
[46] Amos Yong, *The Spirit Poured Out On All Flesh. Pentecostalism and the Possibility of Global Theology* (Grand Rapids: Baker, 2005).

God's acceptance and presence of them in the world.[47] As do Nursi and Gülen, he seeks to engage science and revelation in dialogue rather than disputation. Yong's positions about the Spirit-Wisdom of God as Creator and Revealer may be pursued fruitfully and sympathetically with Gülen and Hizmet. Perhaps Yong's developing theology focused on the Spirit may be linked with the Nursi-Gülen view of Jesus-'Isa's influence for the New Millennium. At least, insha'llah.

Conclusion

Eschatology is important in Christian and Muslim traditions for purposes of inter-religious dialogue and action. The concept of a millennial period between a time of tumult and the final battles is a message for the present. That message is one of hope and challenge for action with an emphasis on renewing creation and providing justice for all persons. Nursi provided a substantial grounding for Gülen, yet Gülen moves the vision and its implementation into the arenas of inter-religious dialogue and joint commitments for the well-being of societies now. Still, Gülen retains eschatological expectations of God's plan being accomplished through those whom God will raise up to lead and live in the world here and now. Küng and, to a greater degree, Yong may be effective partners in carrying on the dialogue.

> Every people have a direction toward which they turn, (a goal they turn to in life and those who turn to the Sacred Mosque have a way they follow to their goal. So strive together as if in a race, towards all that is good. Wherever you may be, God will bring you all together. Surely God has full power over everything. (The Qur'an 2:148)

---

[47] Amos Yong, *Hospitality and the Other. Pentecost, Christian Practices and the Neighbor* (Maryknoll: Orbis Press, 2008).

DIALOGUE BETWEEN RELIGIOUS COMMUNITIES: GÜLEN'S CONTRIBUTION TO ECO-JUSTICE

KARINA KOROSTELINA

In his works on peace, dialogue, and tolerance, Fethullah Gülen stresses the importance of protecting the harmony between the world and humanity. He stresses our responsibility to protect the beauty of the world as well as the foundation that the world provides for humanity, its exquisite mystery. As Gülen explains, "When surrounded with traces, signs, and symptoms that connote these for us, we then become more connected to the present day; we get a deeper sense of our expectations for the future, of our life philosophy and of our past merits."[1] As Gülen repeatedly stresses, to achieve such noble goals, people of different religions and faiths must develop an atmosphere of mutual respect and peaceful co-existence, and engage in dialogue.

This paper analyzes the development of a common overarching identity that can serve as a foundation for dialogue on ecojustice. It uses Fethullah Gülen's approach to dialogue and tolerance as a framework for the development of a dialogue. The paper argues that the development of a common overarching identity of 'humanity' among representatives of all religions develops the possibility of using dialogue as a tool for ecojustice. Such dialogue can lead to the development of a common understanding and shared sense of responsibility to protect the beauty and resources of the world. The paper concludes with a summary of the role of common identity and interfaith dialogue in the promotion of global accountability.

Eco-Justice as a noble goal

In his writings, Gülen stresses that the world that surrounds us does not just provide us with a place for living. It is not just a source of food, water, air and natural recourses. The most important gift of the world is its beauty

---

[1] M. Fetullah Gülen, "Our World and Its Inherently Exquisite Mystery," 2009, http://www.fountainmagazine.com/article.php?ARTICLEID=1071.

reflected in "its inherently exquisite mystery."[2] As Gülen describes "this land of wonders offers beauties of all kinds to us; these are unattainable elsewhere, even in the most beautiful corners of the earth. We feel inundated by the affluence we possess, enchanted by the charm of our accent and in this land we witness so many deeper dimensions that go beyond the material veils of our simple daily chores."[3] The world gives us the possibility to go beyond material interests and to learn about our spirituality, sacred ideas, historical roots, and the path from the past to the future, "our life philosophy and…our past merits."[4]

The preservation of this world is an essential task of humanity. But Gülen goes beyond the idea of the protection and conservation of the world by emphasizing the positive creative force that mankind possesses. He believes that people can bring about positive changes and can transform the world for good: "genuine human beings" can exercise their free will "in a constructive manner, working with and developing the world, protecting the harmony between existence and humanity, reaping the bounties of the Earth and Heavens for the benefit of humanity."[5] Thanks to the efforts of people of good heart, the world can become a better place that rests on the unity of Earth and human beings.

The preservation and positive transformation of the world is a noble goal and a task of good-hearted people. "This is the true nature of a vicegerent and at the same time this is where the meaning of what it is to be a servant and lover of God can be found."[6] To be real protectors of the world, people should be selfless in putting this noble goal above their own aims and inspirations: "selflessness is when one relinquishes oneself from certain personal desires and aspirations, forgoing certain goals associated with property or wealth, and even values associated with one's self-honor and dignity, all for the sake of lofty aims and noble goals."[7] Gülen believes that the responsibility for the common world should become one of the most important goals of humanity. "Gülen…has a clear vision of human greatness, of the traits that define great human beings, those who

[2] Ibid.
[3] Ibid.
[4] Ibid.
[5] Gülen, *Toward a Global Civilization of Love and Tolerance* (New Jersey: The Light, 2004), 124.
[6] Ibid.
[7] Gülen, *Speech and Power of Expression: On Language, Esthetics, and Belief* (Clifton: Tughra Books, 2010).

actualize in themselves the highest and best of human potential."[8] Thus, devotion to the preservation and positive transformation of the world should be a mutual goal and dedication of all human beings. Unfortunately, differences and disagreements between people impede their ability to come together for this noble goal. In the next section I'll discuss how Gülen sees the sources of such disagreements.

Gülen's vision of disagreements between people

Gülen believes that the ability to unite under the common noble goal of protection and positive transformation of the world is obstructed by the global problem of increasing negativity in the perceptions of others. He stresses that "communities and diverse groups within communities live with apparently endless anger, hatred, and detestation, pursuing plans of murder and complete destruction that would never previously been held possible. Nations and all segments within nations wish to get rid of the people or groups that they see as 'other.'"[9] The roots of such negative images, according to Gülen, lie in neglecting positive sides of human relations, humanity and love. The ways people perceive each other are influenced by hate and disgust. "It seems that we have forgotten how to act like human beings...We are overcome with rancor and hatred, flushed with fury, and regard one another with feelings of vengeance. Our breasts are drained of love, a haze of loathing obscures our feelings, and for so many years now the magical aura of love is alien to our perceptions. We constantly produce evil in our thoughts."[10]

In his latest writings, Gülen has stressed that negative images of the Other lead to misperceptions and attribution of unconstructive or aggressive intentions. "Many Muslims, even educated and conscious ones, believe the West seeks to undermine Islam with ever-more subtle and sophisticated methods... Western colonialism is remembered. The Ottoman State collapsed due to European attacks. Foreign invasions of Muslim lands were followed with great interest in Turkey. The gradual 'transformation' of Islam into an ideology of conflict and reaction or into a party ideology also made people suspicious of Islam and Muslims... ."[11] Gülen also describes the negative perception of Muslims: "This negative image has

---

[8] Jill Carroll, *A Dialogue of Civilizations: Gülen's Islamic Ideals and Humanistic Discourse* (New Jersey: The Light, Inc., 2007).

[9] Gülen, "Compassion," *The Fountain* 63 (2008).

[10] Gülen, "Longing for Love," *The Fountain* 64 (2008).

[11] Gülen, *The Necessity of Interfaith Dialogue,* 2002, http://en.fgulen.com/content/view/1053/49/

been fed to the world and now we must once more communicate the essential facet of Islam to those who are presumed to be civilized, using the principle of 'gentle persuasion.'"[12]

Gülen also stresses that the prevalence of emotions over rational vision reduces people's ability to be united by common noble goals. He shows that people who are possessed by anger and hate cannot think and perceive the world rationally: "He or she is paralyzed in terms of faculties, disabled in terms of reasoning, and so lost that she or he can neither think healthily nor can behave normally. Nor is he or she consistent. Bursting into anger, they sometimes destroy and reduce everything around them to ashes, and sometimes they are even in unrelenting rage and fury to the point that they eat out their own heart."[13] In his article "Longing for Love," Gülen further develops this idea. "So many of us act upon our emotions and abandon rational thinking. We trample and silence those who do not think the same as us; this, indeed, is our most distinct character. We plunge forward, headstrong, on our own way, without considering for even a moment that there may be other solutions to different problems; thus, we lead the way to destruction in many cases where we could have been a means for constructive solutions."[14]

The concentration of differences and disagreements impacts emotional reactions and personalities of people making them less open to the inspirations of the common noble goals: "While a person keeps looking at things or events from the perspective of certain considerations, their character and temperament will gradually take shape in line with that way of thinking."[15] Negative views foster negative character traits. Gülen shows that negative thoughts about others, called 'ill-opinion' (sui dhan) are connected with suspicion, jealousy, and rancor. In addition, they lead to self-pride and vanity, concentration on material interests instead of lofty aims and noble goals.[16] People develop tunnel consciousness that rests on their own negative perceptions and restricts their ability to unite toward mutual aspirations: "They never become tired of rancor and cannot get over their anger. Never even attempting to manage their anger, they incessantly run after wickedness, one evil deed after the other, under the

---

[12] Gülen, *Tolerance in the Life of the Individual and Society*, 2004, http://en.fgulen.com/content/view/1800/33/
[13] Gülen, "Compassion," *The Fountain* 63 (2008).
[14] Gülen, "Longing for Love," *The Fountain* 64 (2008).
[15] Gülen, "We Should Think Well of Others," *The Fountain* 64 (2008).
[16] Gülen, "Measure of Selflessness," 2010, http://en.fgulen.com/recent-articles/3608-measure-of-selflessness.html.

influence of these evil thoughts, and they try to make the wrong seem right."[17]

The prevalence of differences and misperceptions in people's minds affects their actions. As Gülen notes, "People's way of thinking shapes their behavior."[18] The results of negative perceptions characterized by hate are violent actions, bombings and murders. "One party carves out the eye of another or murders them; the other responds by running into crowds as suicide bombers or driving a car filled with explosives through them. Violence is everywhere, as savage as, or perhaps even more atrocious than that caused by any barbarian."[19] Thus, even if people are attracted by the noble idea of preservation and positive transformation of the world, they are not capable of working together toward achievement of this goal. The next section discusses ideas for overcoming these problems developed in the framework of social identity theory.

Formation of overarching goals and common identity

According to contact theory in social psychology,[20] the more contacts with representatives of an outgroup a person has, the more positive his or her attitudes toward the outgroup will be. Additionally, the theory recognizes and stresses that simple contact among groups is not sufficient to improve intergroup relations. Several conditions are essential for reducing prejudice and bias: equal status among groups; cooperative intergroup interaction; opportunities for personal acquaintance among group members, especially with those whose personal characteristics do not support stereotypic expectations; and supportive norms by authorities within and outside the contact situation.[21] The effectiveness of these conditions for improving

---

[17] Gülen, "Compassion," *The Fountain* 63 (2008).
[18] Gülen, "We Should Think Well of Others," *The Fountain* 64 (2008).
[19] Gülen, "Longing for Love," *The Fountain*64 (2008).
[20] Gordon Allport, *The Nature of Prejudice* (Cambridge, MA: Addison-Wesley, 1954): Thomas Pettigrew, "Intergroup Contact: Theory, Research and New Perspectives," Annual Review of Psychology 49: 65–85 (1998): Thomas Pettigrew and Linda Tropp, *Does Intergroup Contact Reduce Prejudice? Recent Meta-analytic Findings. In Reducing Prejudice and Discrimination*, ed. S. Oskamp, 93–114. (Hillsdale, NJ: Lawrence Erlbaum. 2000).
[21] Stuart Cook, "Experimenting on Social Issues: The Case of School Desegregation," American Psychologist 40: 452–460 (1985): Thomas Pettigrew, "Intergroup Contact: Theory, Research and New Perspectives," Annual Review of Psychology 49: 65–85 (1998).

intergroup relations has been confirmed in both laboratory and field research.[22]

Some studies provide an explanation of the process of reducing prejudice and bias: changing the nature of interdependence from competition to cooperation and creating opportunities for equal status reduces negative stereotypes toward members of other groups. Conflictual intentions can also be reduced when people experience cognitive dissonance between current positive interactions and previous negative attitudes and stereotypes; as a result, their stereotypes become more positive.[23]

If all conditions are not present, intergroup contact can actually increase prejudice. A study by the National Conference for Community and Justice shows the tendency for increased interaction and contact between racial and ethnic groups from 1993–2000. However, this study also demonstrates the escalation of racial, religious, and ethnic tensions in schools, in neighborhoods, and at work.

The realistic conflict theory clearly demonstrates that contact alone is not sufficient for reducing intergroup conflicts. As I stressed above, this theory not only describes the sources for conflict among groups but also stresses the role of cooperative interdependence and superordinate goals as means toward conflict resolution. It also shows the influence of superordinate identity on the process of conflict mitigation. Cooperative interdependence requires compatible goals; the activity of one party in achieving its goals is useful in achieving another party's goals. There are several types of cooperative interdependence. In some cases it can rest on the basis of social structures and does not require coordination for performing activities. In other cases, a common activity is important for achieving goals. The realistic conflict theory suggests that superordinate goals and positive interdependence are the bases for the development of a common, shared identity. On the contrary, Brewer stresses that a common identity is the foundation for the development of superordinate goals and positive interdependence. In spite of this contradiction, both approaches agree that conflict resolution is possible only in the presence of two conditions: intergroup cooperative activity and common shared identities.

The common identity model developed by Gaertner et al. suggests that cognitive representations of the intergroup context depend on different types of intergroup interaction as well as cognitive, emotional, and social

---

[22] Thomas Pettigrew and Linda Tropp, *Does Intergroup Contact Reduce Prejudice? Recent Meta-analytic Findings. In Reducing Prejudice and Discrimination*, ed. S. Oskamp, 93–114. (Hillsdale, NJ: Lawrence Erlbaum. 2000).
[23] Miller, N., and M. Brewer, eds. *Groups in Contact: The Psychology of Desegregation* (Orlando, FL: Academic Press, 1984).

factors. Changes in these factors can lead to the perception of several groups as one common group, as groups with several subgroups, or as an association of separate individuals. The perception of groups as an association of separate individuals is called decategorization. It can be achieved, for example, by stressing the variation of opinions among ingroup members and some similarities between different opinions of ingroup and outgroup members or by creating more personalized interactions on the basis of personal information.

The perception of several groups as one common group is called supercategorization. It is based on revaluation of former outgroup members as members of a new common ingroup. Supercategorization does not eliminate ingroup favoritism; rather, it readdresses favoritism and leads to the acceptance of former outgroup members. The formation of a new common identity changes people's conceptions of the membership from different groups to a much more inclusive group and makes individual attitudes toward former outgroup members more positive, even in the presence of long-standing antagonism. According to Gaertner et al., this result can be achieved by increasing the importance of common superordinate goals or by introducing new factors such as common tasks or destinies, which are shared by both groups.

The aim of supercategorization is the creation of a new, broader identity that unites groups. New identities can be formed by creating one group with several subgroups. In this case, members of the new group have a dual identity, one of which is connected with the new common group and the other which reflects membership in a subgroup. On the basis of a positive balance of differences and similarities, all members of the new group gain positive attitudes and stereotypes toward others.

As Gaertner et al. show in their studies, an increase in group differentiation, the creation of conditions for cooperative interactions, and the context of interdependence with positive emotional experience are critical factors that influence the formation of a common identity and a subsequent in intergroup prejudice. It is important that members of the new common group have equal status and position within the group. But even if subgroups have different statuses, the dual identity can develop a feeling of commonality and decrease negative attitudes toward members of other subgroups. If people continue to perceive themselves as members of different groups but also feel they are members of a common large group, intergroup relations become more positive when compared to a single ingroup and single outgroup.[24]

Negotiation of a national identity that aims at bringing together previously incompatible identities into a common group is another approach to the development of mutual understanding and inspiration. Such common identity concept must be mutually acceptable and would connect all groups and parties. As Kelman stresses, the capacity to negotiate and change identity rests on two ideas: (1) identities are not zero-sum concepts like territory and resources; and (2) as social constructs, they can be reconstructed and redefined. "In fact, the reconstruction of identity is a regular, ongoing process in the life of any national group. Identities are commonly reconstructed, sometimes gradually and sometimes radically, as historical circumstances change, crises emerge, opportunities present themselves, or new elites come to fore."[25]

Most social identities, especially religious identities, contain some core elements that cannot be negotiated, *e.g* love of God, devotion to sacred ideas, and commitment to religious beliefs. Nevertheless, a few central elements can be reconsidered and redefined while protecting the essential components of identity. To reduce intergroup tensions and develop a common understanding, these elements can be negotiated and discussed during specially organized workshops. Even such identity-based categories as basic needs and conceptions of justice that are often considered non-negotiable can be negotiated because their meaning is dependent on the meaning and structure of ingroup identity. Security, freedom, and community have different senses and are perceived in various ways among people with different social identities. Even for a single person, a basic human need can have various meanings depending on what social identity is most salient at the moment.

The understanding of differences in conceptions of justice, reconciliation, and basic human needs can help to reconcile different identities, even conflictual ones. Identity negotiation workshops include forming a dialogue around differences in the meaning of these basic conceptions and developing ways for their accommodation. Because of variations in perceptions of basic human needs and justice among different

---

[24] John Dovidio and Samuel Gaertner, "Aversive Racism," in Advances in Experimental Social Psychology 36, ed. M. P. Zanna, 1–51 (San Diego: Academic Press, 2004).

[25] Herbert Kelman, "Negotiating national identity and self-determination in ethnic conflicts: The choice between pluralism and ethnic cleansing," *Negotiation Journal* 13 (1997): 338.

groups, it is possible to negotiate these concepts among groups in order to develop a new common identity or reconcile existing identities.

The negotiation of identities is also an important part of the process developing peaceful coexistence between former adversaries. Conflictual identities have to be redefined to accept a new type of intergroup relations and to accept multiple meanings of events. The cooperation of both parties and the step-by-step process of re-creating identity characterized negotiations between postwar France and Germany. These negotiations focused on overcoming a conflictual past and accentuating commonalities through a process of mutual reidentification as "brothers who have engaged in a long fratricidal war."[26]

Thus, social identity theory proposes several approaches to the development of mutual understanding and cooperation: increased contact between people, formation of superordinate goals, development of a common overarching identity, and negotiation of different identities toward a common identity concept. All these approaches rest on the abilities of people to engage in dialogue about their most important mutual issues. The noble goal of preserving and positively transforming the world also depends on the processes and outcomes of interfaith dialogue. In the next section, I'll discuss Gülen's approach to dialogue as described in his works.

Gülen's approach to dialogue

For almost 30 years, the idea of interfaith dialogue has occupied one of the central places in Gülen's works on inter-religious understanding. In his writings and speeches, Gülen has formulated a framework for an Islamic approach to dialogue: "Gülen... has a clear vision of human greatness, of the traits that define great human beings, those who actualize in themselves the highest and best of human potential."[27] Gülen has shown that dialogue between people of different cultures and faiths can bring mutual understanding, respect, and dedication to justice. "Dialogue means the coming together of two or more people to discuss certain issues, and thus the forming of a bond between these people. In that respect, we can call dialogue an activity that has human beings at its axis."[28]

---

[26] For a more in-depth analysis, see Rosoux, "National identity in France and Germany: From mutual exclusion to negotiation," *International Negotiation* 2 (2001).
[27] Carroll, 38.
[28] Gülen, "The Two Roses of Emerald Hill: Tolerance and Dialogue, accessed September 24, 2007, http://en.fgulen.com/content/view/1800/33/.

Dialogue about common goals does not require the acceptance of another group's way of life or values, nor does it necessarily lead to compromise. It offers an opportunity to understand the beliefs, ideas, and positions of others, as well as the basis of their identity. "Accepting all people as they are, regardless of who they are, does not mean putting believers and unbelievers on the same side of the scales. According to our way of thinking, the position of believers and unbelievers has its own specific value... I have such strong feelings and thoughts about him this does not prevent me from entering into dialogue with someone who does not think or believe the same."[29]

Dialogue can further the human ability to come together, forget about previous conflict and misunderstandings, put material interests aside, and work toward a mutual noble goal: "Relationships must be based on belief, love, mutual respect, assistance, and understanding instead of conflict and realization of personal interest. Social education encourages people to pursue lofty ideals and to strive for perfection, not just to run after their own desires. Right calls for unity, virtues bring mutual support and solidarity, and belief secures brotherhood and sisterhood. Encouraging the soul to attain perfection brings happiness in both worlds."[30] Thus, dialogue can serve as an important and crucial tool for the achievement of ecojustice. In the next section, I'll discuss how Gülen's ideas about dialogue can be used to promote the noble goal of the protection and positive transformation of the world.

Dialogue as a tool for achieving ecojustice

The first step in dialogue about the noble goal of ecojustice is the acknowledgement and recognition of the positive side of humanity. In order to alter their negative thinking, people must first recognize and accept their own good nature: "We are far removed from representing our unique status among all of existence. Despite all the qualities we possess which the angels envy, we engage in acts that even evil spirits would be embarrassed of... We are all humans; this means our genes all come from those of Prophet Adam and our essence is from the Truth of Ahmad. Then, come! Let us rise up against all the evil motives and cry out to all the worlds that we are vicegerents on the earth and that we are racing for the

---

[29] Gülen, "A Comparative Approach to Islam and Democracy," accessed September 23, 2007, http://en.fgulen.com/content/view/1027/49/.
[30] Ibid.

heavens! Let us make angels appreciate the eminence of being human!"[31] To Gülen, emphasis on people's good will and good nature is not a new idea: "This is not constructing something from zero point, but revealing things, which were about to be declared 'extinct' despite their existence, and became alien to us due to their inactiveness as reemerging waters in useless holes. We say: 'Human beings are not animals …They are human beings… Therefore, our behaviors should be on a different line and should include different criteria. Our relations with human beings should be based on being human.'"[32]

Such dialogue has to emphasize the positive features in the self-description of an ingroup, such as "being a peaceful people," "valuing tolerance," "open-mindedness and understanding," and "taking pleasure in forgiveness." These images exist in the self-portrayals of all people and serve as powerful sources for self-esteem and pride. As Gülen points out "I can and do say that peace, love, forgiveness, and tolerance are fundamental to Islam."[33] He continues: "Indeed, peace is of the utmost importance to Islam; fighting and war are only secondary occurrences which are bound to specific reasons and conditions. In that respect, we can say that if an environment of peace where all can live in peace and security cannot be achieved in this land, then it would be impossible for us to do any good service for society or for humanity."[34] Thus, the humanity of people can serve as an important basis for a dialogue about the common noble goal of ecojustice.

The emphasis on peaceful images of the ingroup and outgroup can provoke supporting narratives that describe the ingroup's peaceful history and glory and relate positive instances of interethnic relations. Such storytelling by different group members will reinforce these images through complimentary ideas and constructive character. The positive emotions produced during this process will strengthen the formation of peaceful self-concepts and positive perceptions of others, with an emphasis on tolerance, reconciliation, and goodwill. Gülen shows the importance of positive acceptance of the Other, and likewise the importance of avoidance of competition and judgment. "People of heart … open their hearts to everyone, welcoming them affectionately, and appearing as an angel of

---

[31] Gülen, "Longing for Love," *The Fountain* 64 (2008).

[32] Gülen, "An Analysis of the Tolerance Process," accessed September 23 2007, http://www.fethullahgulen.org/recent-articles/1942-an-analysis-of-the-tolerance-process.html.

[33] Gülen, "Dialogue in the Muhammadan Spirit and Meaning," accessed September 25, 2007, http://en.fgulen.com/content/view/1811/33/.

[34] Gülen, "The Two Roses of the Emerald Hills: Tolerance and Dialogue."

preservation in society. Regarding their deeds and attitudes, they try to be compatible with everybody, they try to avoid vicious competition with others, and they avoid resentment... Furthermore, they give generously to other people in pursuit of positive activities and they try to show as much respect as possible to the philosophy and ideas that other people adopt."[35] Moreover, Gülen calls for the perception of others without criticism. Describing people of heart, he shows that "They turn a blind eye to what other people may do wrong. Responding with a smile to those who have displayed negative attitudes, such people nullify bad behavior with kindness, not thinking to hurt anybody, even when they have been hurt over and over again."[36] This perception of others without criticism is a basis for the next step in dialogue: accepting commonality.

The second step of the dialogue concentrates on acknowledgement and acceptance of common values, needs, and goals. This recognition of commonality rests on respect for religion that satisfies and respects the values and needs of all religious groups. Gülen stresses "the necessity of increasing the interests we have in common with other people. In fact, even if the people we talk with are Jews and Christians, this approach still should be adopted and issues that can separate us should be avoided altogether."[37] He also emphasizes that "For interfaith dialogue to succeed, we must forget the past, ignore polemics, and focus on common points."[38] This approach can help resolve contradictions between different groups, changes people's conceptions of a membership in different conflicting groups to membership in a much more inclusive group, and makes attitudes toward other religious groups more positive, even given a long history of offences.

The third step of the dialogue aims at the formation of a common, overarching identity that can establish a foundation for common actions toward the noble goal of ecojustice. Common or shared identities can reduce intergroup hostility by minimizing attention to ethnic/racial/ religious differences and instead creating the sense that all involved are "one unit." Sources for an overarching identity can be found in a common geographic location, common national ideas, shared community problems, and so forth. For example, Gülen shows the similarities of democracy and

---

[35] Gülen, "The Portrait of People of Heart," accessed September 25, 2007, http://www.fethullahGülen.org/recent-articles/2234-the-portrait-of-people-of-heart.html.
[36] Ibid.
[37] Gülen, "Dialogue in the Muhammadan Spirit and Meaning."
[38] Gülen, "The Necessity of Interfaith Dialogue," accessed September 25, 2007, http://en.fgulen.com/content/view/1053/49.

Islam: "In democratic societies, people govern themselves as opposed to being ruled by someone above. The individual has priority over the community in this type of political system, being free to determine how to live his or her own life. Individualism is not absolute, though. People achieve a better existence by living within a society and this requires that they adjust and limit their freedom according to the criteria of social life... As Islam holds individuals and societies responsible for their own fate, people must be responsible for governing themselves."[39]

The formation of a common identity can be reinforced by the discussion of different aspects of the common goal of preservation and positive transformation of the world, including identification of common problems and major issues to address, planning and structuring of activities, developing strategies and tactics, and defining responsibilities. This emphasis on collaboration and cooperation facilitates the creation of narratives of productive partnership, which are based on peaceful concepts and positive images of common group members. The construction of the new common identity must rest on narratives of existent collaborations and situations of successful teamwork. Discussion of such questions as "What can we do together to make our future better?" and "What can we do for our world?" can shift the emphasis of narratives from past opposition to mutual understanding, mutual responsibilities, and the acceptance of the mutual common goal of ecojustice. In this case, the establishment of a peaceful ingroup as a new "We-ness" and devotion to the mutual goal of preservation and positive transformation of the world will develop simultaneously and reinforce each other.

The most important aspect of common identity formation based on common noble goals is that forming this identity does not define a new outgroup or a new enemy to fight. In many instances, people unite under a common overarching identity to defend themselves from a common enemy. In such cases, the new overarching identity is created in opposition to the threat from a new outgroup whose values, needs, core ideas, or actions contradict the values and ideas of the shared identity. Thus, a new cycle of violence can begin as a result of perceived threat to the new overarching identity. In case of the formation of a common identity on the foundation of the noble goal of ecojustice, the people unite to address a common issue, not a common enemy. Thus, this new overarching identity does not produce any more hatred or violence; instead, it unites people toward dignified aims of preservation and positive transformation of the world. It does not draw human energy away to fight a real or imagined

---

[39] Gülen, "A Comparative Approach to Islam and Democracy."

enemy; instead, it produces more human energy by engaging in activities in pursuit of a noble and superior cause.

Conclusion

In his teaching and writing, Gülen introduces the idea of ecojustice as a crucial and noble goal that can unite all people of different faiths and bring about peace in society. "People with different ideas and thoughts are either going to seek ways of getting along by means of reconciliation or they will constantly fight with one another."[40] Gülen sees dialogue as means for this preservation and positive transformation of the world.

Such dialogue includes several discrete and coherent steps that gradually lead to the acceptance and acquisition of the mutual goal of ecojustice. The first step involves acknowledgment and recognition of the humanity and positive inspiration of people. Gülen stresses the importance of emphasizing positive features in the self-description of an ingroup, such as "being a peaceful people," "valuing tolerance," "open-mindedness and understanding," and "taking pleasure in forgiveness." The second step aims at the development of the idea of commonality and acceptance of mutual values, goals and inspirations. Gülen argues that no interfaith dialogue will be successful without increasing interest in the values and ideas that people have in common, and without an understanding of the mutual goals of the mankind. The third step aims at the development of a common overarching identity that can unite all people to address mutual issues. This identity would be based on the reconciliation of past grievances, with an emphasis on future mutual cooperation and peaceful coexistence. Dialogue about the meaning and content of a common national identity also includes discussion of and planning for specific actions of preservation and positive transformation of the world. As Gülen points out, "To conclude, good intentions, positive thinking, and perceiving the beautiful are signs of a person's purity of heart and the immensity of their conscience."[41] His teaching inspires people around the world in engage in interfaith dialogue and develop a common overarching identity that provides a foundation for ecojustice.

---

[40] Gülen, "Tolerance in the life of the individual and society," accessed September 25, 2007, http://en.fgulen.com/content/view/1800/33/.

[41] Gülen, "We Should Think Well of Others," *The Fountain* 64 (2008).

PART 2:

MAKING PEACE BETWEEN HUMANITY AND NATURE

"Sacred Space" and a Coming Religious Peace in the Thought of M. Fethullah Gülen and in the Hizmet Movement

Jon Pahl

In my book *Shopping Malls and Other Sacred Spaces: Putting God in Place*, I explored a Christian "theology of place" that sought to help prevent Christian exploitation of the environment, and to encourage Christians in the practice of eco-justice.[1] The book took up an argument with Saint Augustine, who in his magnum opus *The City of God*, I contend, followed Plato to dislocate (or dematerialize) divine presence in an understandable effort to comfort Christians in the Roman Empire who had just experienced the sack of Rome in 410 CE. After such a trauma, places and space seemed inherently unstable, so Augustine located God primarily in time and event. God acted in and through historical contingencies whose purposes were only dimly perceived, yet which clearly, Augustine argued, transcended mere matter. The City of God was no actual place, or rather it was, as he put it:

> Nature which is not confined to any space but is everywhere in its wholeness. For we say that God is in heaven and earth . . . but that does not mean that we are to say that He has part of himself in heaven and part in earth. He is wholly in heaven, wholly in earth, and that not at different times but simultaneously; and this cannot be true of a material substance.[2]

It is the last line that is the jarring one. If God is immaterial, then is matter merely instrumental? From this dualistic denigration of matter can be read

---

[1] Jon Pahl, *Shopping Malls and Other Sacred Spaces: Putting God in Place* (Grand Rapids: MI: Brazos Press, 2003).
[2] St. Augustine, *The City of God*, tr. Henry Bettenson (NY: Penguin, 1984), bk. 22, ch. 29, 1084.

the long history of Christian exploitation of matter, on behalf of one or another supposedly "spiritual" purpose.

Yet, perhaps it is not too bold to suggest that we have lived with the theological consequences of the sack of Rome long enough. In *Shopping Malls and Other Sacred Spaces* I explored biblical metaphors for divine presence from TANAK and the Christian Covenant for their theological and ecological significance. After all, God is described in *The Holy Bible* as Living Waters, the Light of the World, the Rock of Salvation, the True Vine—and more—in ways that rather clearly contradict, or at least raise questions about, Augustine's dualism. I argue in the book that these metaphors might help reorient Christians toward a more healthy relationship with matter than has been the case in an era when we turned the most minute material into weapons of mass destruction, and when we repeatedly poisoned the waters, air, and earth upon which life depends. In this paper, I will extend my rethinking of sacred space to Islam, through a study of the role of "nature" in the thought of M. Fethullah Gülen and the Hizmet movement inspired by him.

Like Christianity, Islam can seem to favor an event-centered, anti-spatial theology. Muslims resist any "association" of matter with God, reject the Christian doctrine of the incarnation, and feature most notably the activity of God in revelation of *The Holy Qur'an* to the Prophet Muhammad as a central locus for divine presence. This anti-spatial bias in theology can lead to a denigration of matter as merely instrumental, in contrast to "higher" spiritual pursuits. Suicide bombers, for instance, must justify violence to their own bodies in pursuit of some "higher," ostensibly more "spiritual," telos.[3]

And yet, Islam also has a rich spatial tradition, with prayer oriented toward Mecca and the Hajj as central pillars of faith. As I have argued elsewhere, the thought of M. Fethullah Gülen, and the *Hizmet* ("service") movement inspired by him offers an alternative to any anti-material Islam.[4] In what can be depicted as an expanding series of circles, similar to

---

[3] See my "Dying for a Cause: Youth, Violence, and the Gülen Movement— Beyond Tolerance and Dialogue" (paper presented at the Georgetown University Conference on "The Gülen Movement," November 14, 2008). online at http://en.fgulen.com/conference-papers/Gülen-conference-in-washington-dc/3113-dying-for-a-cause-youth-violence-and-the-Gülen-movementbeyond-tolerance-and-dialogue.html

[4] See my essay, "Sacred Space in the *Hizmet* Movement and the Thought of M. Fethullah Gülen" (paper presented at The Gülen Movement: Paradigms, Projects, and Aspirations, The International House at the University of Chicago, November 11-14, 2010).

the whirling dervishes long associated with Turkish culture, sacred space as articulated in several key texts by Gülen and as expressed in practices by those in the *Hizmet* movement, radiates outward from the individual in prayer, through the learning spaces of home and school, to the "spaces" of civil society—including art, poetry, music, and acts of benevolence—and finally to the "spaces" where interreligious dialogue and scientific wisdom about nature come together with spiritual practice. Together, these circles of sacred space form what we might call a secular sacrality, or perhaps a pragmatic mysticism.[5] In the *Hizmet* movement, sacred space is above all moral space. Such a conception of sacred space blends the Sufi and secular histories of Turkey in ways that are negotiated in the details of everyday moral decisions.

In this paper, I will focus on one of those circles, namely the place of "nature," in the thought of Gülen and the *Hizmet* movement. Explicitly, Mr. Gülen asserts that "nature is much more than a heap of materiality or an accumulation of objects: It has a certain sacredness, for it is an arena in which God's Beautiful Names are displayed."[6] Gülen develops this Sufi notion of the sacred space of nature in several directions, and those Muslims inspired by him have applied his thinking in practical action that demonstrates concern for the environment as a moral responsibility of Muslims, indeed, of all human beings, and that points us toward what I call "a coming religious peace."

I.

Most notably, the Hizmet movement clearly emphasizes "scientific" education and care for the environment. Gülen writes: "There can be no conflict among the Qu'ran, the Divine Scripture, . . . the universe, . . . and the sciences." Gülen quotes Bediüzzaman, or Said Nursi—the early 20th century Muslim scholar who is an inspiration for him—who said that the best education "sees the illumination of the mind in science and knowledge, and the light of the heart in faith and virtue."[7] Many of the

---

[5] The notion of expanding circles of sacred space is developed by Seth Kunin in an article on "Judaism," in *Sacred Place: Themes in Religious Studies,* ed. Jean Holm with John Bowker (London/NY: Pinter, 1994), 115-148. It is also a famous metaphor developed by Rainer Maria Rilke, *The Book of Hours,* tr. Annemarie S. Kidder (Evanston, IL: Northwestern University Press, 2001), 3.

[6] Gülen, *Essays-Perspectives-Opinions*, 83.

[7] Gülen, *Toward a Global Civilization of Love and Tolerance* (Somerset, NJ: The Light), 196-7.

schools founded by members of the Hizmet movement put this principle into practice as "science academies."

Gűlen envisions a harmony between faith and reason, where we discover that "science and religion [are] two manifestations of the same truth."[8] This is akin to what Lutheran pastor, theologian, medical missionary, and Nobel Peace Prize laureate Albert Schweitzer called an ethic of "reverence for life." "Life," Gűlen suggests, "is the foremost and most manifest blessing of God Almighty."[9] Consequently, to understand life through science is nothing less than to enter a sacred place. At its best, "science . . . in truth should be considered as holy as a temple."[10]

At the same time that he extols scientific understanding of nature, Gűlen is realistic about the limits of science. "Science and technology," he writes,

can turn the world into a hell in the hands of an irresponsible minority. . . . We have to ask in whose service science and technology are today. . . . Do they encourage sharing, abstinence from exploitation, respect for basic human rights and freedoms or do they serve the sovereignty of capital and crude force?[11]

Without such connection to ethical purposes or ends, in which matter is understood as more than instrumental, science has led us to an age of "global environmental disasters," an age in which "a quarter of the world does not have access to healthy drinking water," and an age in which caring for the health of one another "has become an industry with very expensive services."[12]

In the final analysis, however, and as the curricular offerings of the many schools associated with Mr. Gűlen suggest, science is as holy as a temple, a veritable sacred place, when it is directed toward humane, moral goals. Gűlen writes:

Science and technology and the speed with which they allow us to perform are sacred and worthy of respect only in proportion with how much they direct humans toward humane goals, facilitate the accomplishment of these goals . . . bring about peace and happiness . . ., participate in the

---

[8] Ibid., 82.
[9] Ibid., 63.
[10] Ibid., 142.
[11] Ibid., 235-6.
[12] Ibid., 195, 236, 237.

resolution of worldly and spiritual problems and give momentum to research . . . [to] enhance our understanding.[13]

Once again, sacred space in the Hizmet movement is, first and foremost, moral space. And thus the relations between scientists (and engineers) and nature are not merely the relations between humans and brute matter. They are morally charged relationships that must, in the end, serve not only capital and brute force but must serve truth—both empirical and theological.

II.

So, Gülen and members of the Hizmet movement directly advocate for scientific study of nature as a sort of moral entry into a sacred place. More indirect, but perhaps even more important, are the ways that crucial metaphors found in the theology of the movement orient members toward nature as sacred space. Much theology, of course, is poetry.[14] Metaphors matter. Metaphors matter in quiet ways; they operate largely subconsciously (like poetry, music, and other forms of art) to fashion desires and to forge values. And the metaphors Gülen uses to describe divine presence, and to describe the ideal relationships of people of faith to God and to one another, are often nature-centered.

For instance, many of the schools built by members of the Hizmet movement feature "Light" in their names. This metaphor refers to God, of course, but also serves as a constant reminder that the energy without which people cannot live is a gift of the Creator. Enlightenment is the goal, or illumination, as Gülen explains in a passage describing his philosophy of education:

A new style of education that fuses religious and scientific knowledge with morality and spirituality will produce genuinely enlightened people with hearts illuminated by religious sciences and spirituality, minds illuminated by positive sciences, characterized by all kinds of humane merits and moral values, and cognizant of the socio-economic and political conditions of their time.[15]

Such people will produce a "springtime," a time of light, or a "golden generation."

---

[13] Ibid., 235-6.
[14] See, for instance, Sallie McFague, *Models of God: Theology for an Ecological, Nuclear Age* (Philadelphia: Fortress Press, 1987).
[15] Gülen, *Toward a Global Civilization of Love and Tolerance,* 231-2.

Just as "light" is a crucial metaphor in the movement for divine presence in life, so too goes Gülen utilize other nature metaphors to describe how a relationship with God works. For instance, Gülen describes the "Prophet Muhammad, peace and blessings be upon him, [as] like a spring of pure water in the heart of a desert, a source of light in an all-enveloping darkness."[16] Faith in the heart of believers enables them to "plant new saplings everywhere," "plant roses with determination," and at the same to "stand like mountains against the most pitiless attacks."[17] Such metaphors mirror the model of power that the medieval Christian mystic Hildegard of Bingen called "viriditas," or "greening power." According to Bingen, God's power is like the power of growing or greening things. For her, Jesus was the ultimate "green one," because like any "true vine," it was Jesus' *death* on the cross that brought new *life* in the springtime of resurrection.[18] Similar metaphors in the writings of Gülen serve to remind movement members that nature is a gift, rather than mere matter, and that it is therefore the responsibility of humans to protect the gift, rather than to use it for destructive or exploitative purposes.

Even more importantly, Gülen describes nature itself as a domain of love. Consequently, all of nature, and especially the body and care for the body, participates in the Sacred who *is* loving compassion and mercy. Too little attention has been paid to the work of Hizmet movement participants in the arenas of healthcare and healing, where (obviously) skill and creativity in natural sciences and spiritual love might intersect. "Creation is the result of lighting the wick of the candle of love," Gülen writes, "the wick of 'being known and seen.' If the Lord did not love creation, there would be neither moons, nor suns nor stars. The heavens are all poems of love, with the Earth being the rhyme."[19] Nature thus points us toward our interrelatedness, and moves us beyond any dualism. Gülen goes on: "As we are all limbs of the same body, we should cease this duality that violates our very union."[20] Such compassion enables people of faith to act

like each others' eyes and ears, tongue and lips, hands and feet. In this society, every individual has devoted themselves to facilitate another's life, to do all that they can for the happiness of others. . . . When one is hurt, all

---

[16] Ibid., 64.

[17] Ibid., 107-9.

[18] See, for instance, Stephanie Roth, "The Cosmic Vision of Hildegard of Bingen," *The Ecologist* (January 2000), accessed October 27, 2010, http://findarticles.com/p/articles/mi_m2465/is_1_30/ai_59520592/?tag=content;col1.

[19] Gülen, *Toward a Global Civilization of Love and Tolerance*, 5.

[20] Ibid., 7.

the others feel this pain in their hearts. All join in the feast of happiness when one partakes of it.[21]

Gülen here articulates an insight common to many peacemakers. Dr. Martin Luther King, Jr. famously put it this way in his *Letter from Birmingham City Jail:* "Injustice anywhere is a threat to justice everywhere."[22] Vietnamese Buddhist peace activist Thich Nhat Hanh puts it like this: "'To be' is to inter-be. We cannot just *be* by ourselves alone. We have to inter-be with every other thing."[23] And that noted Jewish rabbi, Jesus of Nazareth, put it this way: "Whatever you do to the least of these among you, you have done it to me."[24] Every place in nature, and especially every human being, participates in the dignity of the Sacred. "We need pure and virtuous people," Gülen contends, "who can read the verses of God in the faces of people."[25]

From these metaphors, drawn especially from the Sufi approach to Islam, Gülen opens up the entire world of nature to sacred presence:

> When love meets the heart, people always think of [God], speak to [God] in the inner world and taste [God's] blessings, openly and explicitly, in the water they drink, in the food they taste and in the air they breathe. Moreover, they feel the warmth of [God's] intimacy in all actions. . . . This road is open to everybody.[26]

In language that evokes the experiential mysticism of many theologians, believers "taste" God in the loving gifts of the natural world.

Needless to say, then, a nature infused with love impels human beings toward moral responsibility, and especially toward non-violence. "Every aspect of the universe's mind-boggling beauty, grandeur, and splendor is an example of God's artistry," Gülen claims. "In this respect," he goes on:

> humans, animals, other animate creatures, and, in fact, all the inanimate objects as well, were created with a nature that is worthy of being embraced by us with love. Showing indifference or being condescending to them means showing indifference and acting with condescension to the

---

[21] Ibid., 163.

[22] Martin Luther King, Jr., "Letter from Birmingham City Jail," in *A Testament of Hope: The Essential Writings and Speeches of Martin Luther King, Jr.*, ed. James M. Washington (SF: HarperCollins, 1986), 289.

[23] Thich Nhat Hanh, *Peace is Every Step: The Path of Mindfulness in Everyday Life* (NY: Bantam, 1991), 96.

[24] Matt 25:40

[25] Gülen, *Toward a Global Civilization of Love and Tolerance,* 12.

[26] Ibid., 13.

Maker. On the contrary, our approach to creation and other human beings should be based on loving them for the sake of their Creator. If Muslims talk about weapons, armories, killing and butchering of others . . . then this means that in fact we have been far removed from our essence.[27]

Even "jihad," so often misunderstood and mischaracterized in Western media, Gülen describes with an organic metaphor. "All efforts made to reform society and people are part of jihad," or part of the responsibility of believers to "bear fruit." "Believers, like trees, can survive only as long as they bear fruit."[28] When we are capable of seeing even inanimate nature as infused with sacred presence and love, and when we recognize spiritual struggle in light of the organic (and nonviolent) commandment to "bear fruit," then we will not heedlessly destroy nature with weapons of mass destruction or ecological degradation.

Finally, these metaphors that find love at the heart of the natural world, or that see nature as sacred space, imply a commitment to justice. This will not come easily. Any birth requires labor. "What lies at the roots of the behavior of people of service," as Gülen articulates it, "is a long period of preparation and severe suffering followed by an appeal to mercy aimed at a search for human rights." Hizmet people "are the leaders in each and every charitable act," and "they are people of this world and the next, people whose contact with others . . . can be considered as contact with God. Apparently, it is possible to observe the zenith of the Hereafter from this sort of worldliness."[29] This secular sacrality, or pragmatic mysticism, locates divine presence in acts of mercy and justice:

Over and above the maxim, "Desire not for others what you do not desire for yourself," such people ceaselessly try harder for others so that others will benefit from what these people of heart have already found useful. With the boundlessness of the horizon of such people, they are able to revive the feeling of mercy in the hearts of tyrants. At the same time, they believe that being with the oppressed is the same as being with God, and thus support them.[30]

This quest for justice has an ascetic component. Living on behalf of justice means living with some limits: a God-follower "limits personal desires and passions."[31] Yet the result is boundless courage and capacity to recognize

---

[27] Ibid., 46-7.
[28] Ibid., 172.
[29] Ibid., 22.
[30] Ibid., 23.
[31] Ibid., 102.

the possibility of *tikkun olam*, repair of the world's injustices: "Even if there were no real people left on Earth, even if all the horizons were obscured by dust, even if the streets had been invaded by total depravity, even if the thorns were to outnumber the roses. . . [people of service] would still stand unshakable and say," according to Gűlen

> I stand even though all the others have collapsed! Everywhere may turn to desert. But since I have my tears for moisture, it is not a problem. God has given me two feet on which to walk and two hands with which to work. I have belief as my capital, and my territory is as vast as my heart. Opportunities to restore the world are awaiting me.[32]

III.

So, nature as sacred space among people of *Hizmet* motivates scientific inquiry, and tempers technological grandiosity, by situating nature within a cosmos infused by divine presence as articulated in rich metaphors linking nature and grace and pushing humanity towards moral responsibility. One of the most intriguing, and controversial, ways that this Sufi-inspired understanding of sacred space is present among those inspired by Fethullah Gűlen is in their appreciation for music and the arts, along with other forms of natural sociability and participation, including entrepreneurial activity on behalf of justice and the common good.

As is well known, the Hizmet movement embraces not only "professional" theologians, but also "lay" professionals—engineers, financiers, economists, physicians, and more. These volunteers often integrate in their vocations the practice of natural sciences with religious commitment in a social movement. They also contribute in practical ways to projects on behalf of justice. The social movement organization, *Kimse Yok Mu*, is only the most notable example of this spirit of service that finds expression in disaster relief and compassionate accompaniment of, and aid to, those who suffer. But in the schools, research labs, academic appointments, hospitals, and many other "secular" vocations, people of service apply spiritual values in various forms of social entrepreneurship. It will be interesting to see, in coming decades, whether individuals inspired by Gűlen will move to the forefront of so-called "green industries," or will develop environmentally-friendly corporations who manage to bridge "doing good" with "doing well." Perhaps individuals inspired by Hocaefendi, or "respected teacher," as he is affectionately dubbed in the movement, have already innovated in this arena in ways of

---

[32] Ibid., 110.

which I'm unaware. Certainly the principles of Gülen, and especially his notion of "harmony," pose no obstacle to the development of social entrepreneurial agencies on behalf of "greening power."

For Gülen, "harmony" is nothing less than a synonym for Islam. He writes:

> Submission, the state of being a subject of God in its broadest sense, is the celestial title of being in harmony with existence and things, of being well-adjusted to the world and all that is in it, of making one's way through the mysterious hallways of the universe without getting lost, in short, of protecting the balance of one's inner harmony with existence.[33]

Harmony and balance imply, of course, making constant adjustments to the contingencies of life and history, and being aware of the manifold interconnections of an individual existence with the cosmos.

Consequently, music is an apt metaphor to elucidate this reality of Islam. Gülen frequently refers to music in his own writings, and many gatherings of people of Hizmet feature musical performances, often of extraordinary virtuosity. Music, of course, transcends the parochial languages of speech in ways that can unite people in an aural sacred space—a sense of the presence of a beauty *heard* that points toward the eternal. Succinctly, people around the globe love music, and this love is of God. Gülen writes:

> The most dominant factor in the spirit of existence is love. As an individual of the universal chorus, almost every creature acts and behaves in its own style, according to the magical tune it has received from God, in a melody of love. . . . From this perspective, humankind "consciously" participates in this symphony of love that is being played in existence.[34]

In my own research on sacred space, I similarly described the "city of God" imagined in the *Book of Revelation* as the sound of participation that making and hearing a "gospel choir" can invoke. All those choirs of angels of many bad jokes might actually have something to recommend them.

If music can reveal the harmony of Islam, and an aural sacred space, so too can other arts, including literature, poetry, and the visual arts. Again, this trajectory in *Hizmet* is controversial; people have killed and died in conflicts over icons and visual representations. Tolerance would seem to mark the Hizmet movement, and Gülen himself clearly recognizes the power of art. He writes: "It is art which inspires human beings to travel in

---

[33]Ibid., 123.
[34]Ibid., 9.

the depths of oceans and heavens. By means of art, humanity sets sail for the outer limits of the Earth and sky and reaches feelings beyond time and space."[35] To be sure, Gűlen grounds this appreciation for visual art in classical Islamic forms. "It was by means of art combined with faith," he writes, that enabled Islam

> with its magnificent places of worship, slender minarets pointing to the realms beyond; sacred designs and intricate patterns carved in marble each of which served a distinct message; diverse kinds of calligraphy, brilliant gildings; and embroideries as beautiful and fine as butterfly wings, that this once magnificent world of Islam became a gallery of invaluable beauty.[36]

If nature is sacred space, then the artist's attempt to communicate that reality, whether in music, poetry, or the visual arts—deserves respect.

* * *

As recent events surrounding the so-called Ground Zero mosque reveal, sacred space is often controverted space.[37] Especially here in the U.S., one trajectory of the American civil religion tends to fixate on places to memorialize the American dead—Washington Monument, Gettysburg Battlefield, the Vietnam Veterans Memorial, and now the World Trade Center site. There are historical reasons for this tendency that I do not have time to go into today, which I have taken to calling "thanatopophilia."[38]

Within the *Hizmet* movement, a very different conception of sacred space would seem to emerge. As I have argued here, and elsewhere, sacred space in the *Hizmet* movement is above all moral space. Yet included within the scope of moral action, because it reflects the presence of a living, compassionate, and merciful (though inscrutable) God, is nature. People of service can engage with the natural world fully, without hesitation, because nature "has a certain sacredness . . . [as] an arena in which God's Beautiful Names are displayed." This means that scientific inquiry can be exploration of sacred space, and that theological metaphors reflecting the harmony and beauty of the natural world are appropriate.

---

[35] Gülen, *Pearls of Wisdom,* tr. Ali Ünal (NJ: The Light, 2006), 66.
[36] Ibid.
[37] See on this theme David Chidester and Edward T. Linenthal, eds., *American Sacred Space* (Bloomington and Indianapolis: Indiana University Press, 1995).
[38] See for instance, Drew Gilpin Faust, *This Republic of Suffering: Death and the American Civil War* (NY: Knopf, 2008).

Even more—human relationships with nature are something more than merely exploitative domination of brute matter.

This conception of nature as sacred space has profound implications for global justice and peace. Indirectly, at least, as we (re)discover and live with the deep metaphors that locate divine presence in the material and contingent world, we might be motivated to act morally in study and service to help remedy some of the damage done to the environment in previous generations.[39] Even more directly, while many commentators have focused on the political implications of the Hizmet movement, I suspect its potential contributions to global environmental justice, flowing from this sense of nature as sacred space, and as put into practice by scientists, engineers, and social entrepreneurs, may prove even more significant. Such contributions will help build what I call, in my forthcoming book, "a coming religious peace."[40] For this conception of sacred space as moral space, expressed in responsibility for the shared gifts of this one blue and green planet that we share, is something that our enduring religious traditions—if not the American civil religion (although there is a minority strand of that tradition that might be mobilized, too)— can actually come to advocate for together.

---

[39] Muhammed Çetin, *The Gülen Movement: Civic Service without Borders* (NY: Blue Dome, 2009) and Helen Rose Ebaugh, *The Gülen Movement: A Sociological Analysis of a Civic Movement Rooted in Moderate Islam* (Heidelberg: Springer, 2010).

[40] See Jon Pahl, *Empire of Sacrifice: The Religious Origins of American Violence* (NY: New York University Press, 2010).

FETHULLAH GÜLEN AND ECO-JUSTICE: FROM GENESIS 1:28 AND QUR'AN 2:30 TO PLATONIC ERGON AND ARISTOTELIAN HARMONIA

ORI Z. SOLTES

Like the Pillars of Islam, this chapter will offer five components. It will begin by considering scriptural passages from both Jewish, Christian and Muslim sacred texts that reflect on the shaping of humanity with respect to our relationship to each other and to the world around us. What do biblical passages such as Genesis 1:28-30 and 2:19-20, and qur'anic passages such as *Al-Baqara* (Q 2:30) and *Adh-Dhariyat* (Q 51:56), instruct us regarding those relationships? How are we intended by God to act vis-à-vis each other and the world?

The paper will turn to a brief discussion of how Plato's thought distinguishes *logos*—discussion—from *ergon*: action; of what Aristotle means by the term *harmonia*—the bringing of apparently opposed ideas into dynamic synthesis; and of how the Platonic and Aristotelian perspectives differ with regard to the human approach to the world around us.

Finally—and this will be the primary focus and the ultimate purpose of this chapter—the discussion will focus on three essays by Fethullah Gülen. "Humanity and Its Responsibilities," "An Ideal Society," and "The Meaning of Life" all contribute to a world view that both explicitly and implicitly draws from the threefold Abrahamic tradition with respect to human-human and human-natural world relations and does so by applying principles expressed by Plato and Aristotle—specifically the ideas of *logos, ergon* and *harmonia.*

This essay is thus both an analysis of Gülen's thinking with respect to the matter of eco-justice—how, specifically, he synthesizes elements of Jewish, Christian, Muslim, Platonic and Aristotelian thought—and an articulation of how Gülen's thinking offers a paradigm—that paradigm is *hizmet*—for being-in-the-world, for the movement that bears his name and the larger world in which that movement offers a positive influence.

***

Barely have the first humans been created, as that process is recounted in the biblical book of Genesis, and God "blessed them and God said unto them: 'Be fruitful and multiply, and fill the earth and subdue it; and have dominion over the fish of the sea, and over the birds of the air, and over every living thing that creeps upon the earth.'"[1] The obvious question raised by God's words is: what do the terms "subdue" and "dominion"— translations of Hebrew words, *k-v-sh* and *r-d-h*—actually *mean*? How are we to understand what God has in mind for Adam and Eve and for us, their descendants? More to the point: given the inherent and paradoxic difficulty of ever knowing exactly what God means by *any* words, since God is by definition an entity different from us—even as God has created us (and thus may be assumed to have a direct connection to us, within us)—how are we to interpret these words?

One means of interpreting is to look at the words in the larger context in which they appear. Thus for instance, in the verses immediately preceding Gen 1:28 we read "And God said: 'Let us make humans in our own image, after our likeness; and let them have dominion over the fish of the sea, and over the birds of the air, and over every creeping thing that creeps upon the earth.' (1:26) and (1:27): "God created humans in His own image, in the image of God He created them; male and female He created them." From this it seems reasonable to infer that "subdue" and "dominion" are intended to be behaviors that emulate God, whose power gives Him ultimate dominion over all of reality, which is in its entirety subject to Him.

This in turn begets the question: how does God enact His power over the universe, including humans? For one thing, God operates out of a purely spiritual (as opposed to physical) state of being. Moreover, we understand from another nearby verse—2:7—that God "breathed into its nostrils the breath of life (*nishmat hayyim*); and [thus] the human became a living soul (*nefesh hayyah*)." Thus there is something of God within us, and that something is the spiritual component that animates the otherwise lifeless physical being created from earth.[2] So one implication of 1:28 is that the spiritual should conquer the physical – that the mind and the soul should have dominion over the material part of ourselves and of the world around us.

---

[1] Gen 1:28

[2] The word "animate" derives from the Latin "*anima*," which means "soul"—it effectively translates "*nefesh.*" The word "Adam" derives from the Hebrew "*adamah*," meaning "earth."

Moreover, as we struggle to put the Creator into terms and concepts that we can understand, we observe of God the exercise of a parental capacity to guide as He governs, to push and pull while permitting us a full exercise of the Free Will that is apparently inherent—and thus God-given—within us. Even when Adam and Eve choose to abrogate a direct divine commandment with respect to eating fruit from a particular tree in the Garden of Eden, the all-knowing, all-powerful God does not intervene to stop them. Their action becomes a layered learning experience: there are consequences for our actions—in this case, fairly severe consequences. But the consequences are never so extreme that Adam and Eve or their descendants are destroyed by them; the consequences fall within the range of what we can sustain, if not always comfortably.

The handing over of responsibilities for caretaking the world around us, of considering not just what, with respect to fish and fowl and creeping animals, serves our own needs, but what serves *their* needs as well, may certainly be inferred, then, from the juxtaposition of Gen 1:26-7 with Gen 1:28-30. We might see this inference further validated by the verses that follow shortly, in 2:19-20. There, sandwiched between the two parts of the specific accounting of how the first human became two—the decision to create a helpmate for Adam and the process by which that deed was accomplished—we read that "out of the ground the Lord God formed every beast of the field, and every bird of the air; and brought them unto the human to see what he would call them; and whatsoever the human would call every living creature that was to be the name thereof. And the human gave names to all cattle and to the birds of the air and to every beast of the field…"

So just as parents name their children, Adam names the other creatures around him. And as such, the responsibility for these other creatures may be understood to echo that of a parent for his or her children—which echoes that of God for us. Moreover, with the distinction between all of these creatures among whom "there was not found a helpmate for [Adam]" (2:20) and Eve, who is created as that helpmate, we can further understand how humans—specifically, both males and females; "bone of my bones and flesh of my flesh" (2:23)—are to be treated: as equal partners in shouldering the responsibilities that come with parenthood, not only of our own human children but of the world around us.

"Subjection" and "dominion," like the act of naming, then, are to be understood as terms that don't merely empower us to assert our will over the world around us but as imperatives to use our power to shepherd the world, engaging in constant efforts to improve and even to hope to perfect it in partnership with the God who, by ceding to us free will, has invited that partnership. And that partnership includes all humans, both as heirs to the first humans in the Garden and, in practical terms, as all endowed as co-equal recipients of divine intentions and commands, and co-equal bearers of the responsibility implied by these biblical passages.

Many generations after the biblical text was written down, and the two forms of faith that look to it as the ultimate connector—a verbal umbilicus between God and humanity—had been shaped as Judaism and Christianity, a third sibling to these two was shaped by the Prophet Muhammad. The words that, transmitted through the Prophet to his constituents, form the ultimate umbilical connector between God and humanity for Islam are contained within the text of the Qur'an. Not surprisingly, we find the same matter of human dominion and responsibility that is engaged in the biblical book of Genesis also engaged in the Qur'an.

Thus in the second *sura* (chapter) of the Qur'an, known as *Al-Baqara* ("The Heifer"), we read (in verse 29): "And when the Lord said unto the angels, 'I am about to place a vice-regent in the earth,' they said, 'Will you place therein one who will do evil therein and shed blood?'" So we encounter here, too, the notion of a particular status for humankind vis-à-vis the world, but with variations on both the context details—the conversation between God and the angels, which is not present as a feature of the Genesis account—and more importantly, the key word in the proposal and the concern expressed by the angels. Thus in lieu of the verbs "subject" and "have dominion" the Qur'an provides us with the noun, "vice-regent."

The Arabic term rendered as "vice-regent" is *khalifa*. One might see this as a gloss on the Genesis narrative. The Qur'an makes more explicit the position of humankind between God and other creatures, of acting on God's behalf toward them. For what does a vice-regent—a deputy; a caliph—do? He serves in place of the regent when the latter is not available, seeks to carry out what the regent's actions would be were he present—and must answer to the regent for whatever those actions are, resulting either in approval or disapproval for them.

There are at least two contextual details that intensify our interest in this Qur'anic passage, both in and of itself and in comparison with the biblical passage. One of these details is the previously-noted idea of God's sharing His intentions with the angels. Interestingly, while this is not found in Genesis, in the Jewish literature that discusses and interprets the biblical material—the *midrash rabba*—the rabbis ask why it is that in Gen 1:26 the pronoun and verb are in the plural: "let *us* make humans in *our* own image." Within the lengthy *midrash* discussion, one commentator,

Rabbi Simeon, suggests that this refers to God's discussion with the ministering angels.

So it is as if the Qur'an has absorbed this elucidatory information and embedded it within its text.[3] Moreover, the *midrash* represents the ministering angels as arguing about whether or not God should create humans at all, based on the assertion either that "they will perform righteous deeds" or that "they are full of strife." The latter sensibility—which would seem to anticipate all of the negative human actions that follow from disobeying God's command regarding the fruit from the tree—is also encompassed by the Qur'anic passage.

In sura 51—the chapter of "The Scatterers" (*Adh-Ddhariyat*)[4]—we also read, regarding the creation of human beings, that "I have not created the jinn and humankind except that they may worship me: I do not desire any provision from them, and I do not wish them to feed me..."[5] Thus the text of God's word to the Prophet reminds us that not only does God not require from us food—offerings—since God is in fact the ultimate provider of food and everything else: "Verily, God, He is the provider, endowed with steady might..."(v 58) —but that we need to define our existence in terms of the proper spiritual turn toward God ("...that they may worship me...") rather than material gestures that are pointless in and of themselves.

If the two Qur'anic passages are placed not only in their immediate contexts, but side by side, then we may recognize that the Divine intention is for us to turn toward Him for guidance, and to emulate God in our conduct to other humans and to the larger world around us as a most effective means of turning toward God. To function effectively as God's vice-regent is both to behave as God would toward all of creation—provided and created and surely loved by God—and in an appropriately worshipful manner toward God. And it is to place spiritual focus above material interests.

---

[3] We can understand this in two different ways: that the Prophet was privy to *midrash* shared with him by the rabbinic figures with whom he had conversations in Mecca and Yathrib/Medina; and/or that in the revelation to him, God offered fuller details than had either been offered to Moses in the first place or retained within the Torah over time. The first would be a Jewish/Christian perspective, the second a Muslim perspective—but neither perspective necessarily precludes the other.

[4] The title of this sura is also rendered as "The Lashing Gales," or as "The Winnowing Winds."

[5] The Qur'an 51:56-7

***

Thus we may understand all three Abrahamic traditions as offering distinct prescriptions regarding how humankind should operate vis-à-vis the world. These prescriptions, with variations of detail, obligate us to function as God does, albeit, obviously, on a more modest scale, in shepherding, protecting and promoting the well-being of it all—from the grass at our feet to the upper reaches of our own being in our most august aspects—and to favor the spiritual aspect of ourselves that distinguishes us from other physical beings.

It is this theme and the related ramifications of these scriptural passages that Fethullah Gülen takes up a number of times in his writings. No places exhibit this focus more eloquently and intensely than his essays, ""Humanity and Its Responsibilities," "The Horizons of Tranquility," "An Ideal Society," "The Meaning of Life"—and also "Educational Services Are Spreading Throughout the World." Gülen's starting point in the first of these five works is to consider the matter of human vice-regency: "If humanity is the viceregent of God on earth... then the Divine Being that has sent humanity to this realm will have given us the right, permission and ability to discover the mysteries imbedded in the soul of the universe... to be the representatives of characteristics that belong to Him, such as knowledge, will and might."[6]

One of Gülen's particular emphases throughout his writings is on the importance of science and the falseness of the proposition that science and faith inherently contradict each other. We can recognize that specific aspect of his focus in his reference to the mysteries imbedded in the soul of the universe—a turn of phrase that is at once drawn from a spiritual vocabulary but in line with the stated and unstated goals of biology, physics, medicine—in short any and all scientific disciplines that seek into the minutest subatomic elements within the universe, that seek out toward the most unfathomably distant elements of outer space, and that seek to unravel the human genome and to relieve human suffering.

This connection is overtly articulated in the second paragraph of the essay, where Gülen observes that "[i]t is clear that with the success and accomplishments that have been achieved up until today people have been sent to the world with specific instruments and opportunities... We have changed the world by developing it, and wittingly or not, we are the mirror

---

[6] Fethullah Gülen, "Humanity and Its Responsibilities," in *Toward a Global Civilization of Love and Tolerance* (Somerset, NJ: The Light, Inc., 2006), 204.

that reflects the new cadre described when the Great and Just One stated *I will create a viceregent on Earth.*"[7]

Moreover, Gülen specifically and directly connects Sura 2:30 with 51:56—he renders the phrase that I have quoted above as "that they may worship me" as "that they may act as my subjects"—which, in the context of the God-given skills possessed by humans, through which we have accomplished so much, is a "clear statement [that] is both a call for communal responsibility and a call for giving thanks for the things that have been bestowed on humanity." When our conduct protects the earth and its inhabitants, it is conduct that both glorifies and gives thanks to God.[8]

Part of what makes it possible for us to conduct ourselves in this manner is the recognition that not only are we subject to God but our primary spiritual obligation is to submit to God. When we function as *muslims*—those who submit to God's will; the term with a miniscule, rather than majuscule "m" refers to a range of individuals of diverse spiritual traditions, from Abraham to ourselves, who dedicate themselves to such submission—then we are "in harmony with existence and things…well-adjusted to the world and all that is in it, ….protecting the balance of [our] inner harmony with existence." Further, "[t]he success of humankind in protecting their relationship with existence and the physical world can be determined by the degree to which they act in accordance with the purpose of all of creation."[9]

Thus there is a distinct connection between our protection of each other and the world around us—our acts of justice and eco-justice—and our relationship to God mediated by God's word. Far from offering contradictions of each other, spirituality and science can and should yield a splendid interface, when the latter functions in harmony with the physical universe as opposed to seeking to subject it to an egotistical form of human will. Moreover, part of our inevitable, God-given, human nature—part of our condition of divinely-appointed vice-regency, tied to the God-given possession of free will—is our curiosity. That curiosity encompasses our desire to know and understand God. And one of the obvious paths to such knowledge and understanding is the exploration of all of God's creation. Gülen continues:

> Humanity's viceregency for the Creator takes place in an unusually broad sphere that encompasses acts ranging from believing in Him and

---

[7] Ibid., 205.
[8] Ibid., 206.
[9] Ibid., 206.

worshipping Him to understanding the mysteries within things and the
cause of natural phenomena...[G]enuine human beings try to exercise
their freewill in a constructive manner, working with and developing the
world, protecting the harmony between existence and humanity... This is
the true nature of a viceregent and at the same time this is where the
meaning of what it is to be a servant and lover of God can be found.[10]

Throughout the remainder of "Humanity and Its Responsibilities," Gülen
continues to reinforce and elaborate on the details of how the combination
of eager exploration of the physical universe and proper protection of it as
we develop its resources, offer a primary mode of worship of and
submission to God, one that in offering "the clearest expression of the
relationship amongst humans, the universe, and God" fulfills the
obligations of our vice-regency and offers the potential of transforming
our world into the Eden from which our aboriginal ancestors were forced
to depart: "[Genuine humans] will walk in the greatest spiritual ecstasy,
overstepping the boundaries of existence and reaching Eden."[11]

He directly echoes this view in any number of other essays. For
example, in "The Horizons of Tranquility," he notes regarding those who
turn toward God in submission to the Divine Will, that they "feel the
vastness of the title of viceregent which has been bequeathed to them...sip
water, breath air and accept all manners of presents as blessings from God.
They inhale the scent of the earth and those to which it gives birth as if it
were the sweetest of aromas. They salute the orchards and gardens, the
mountains and valleys, the grasses and trees, the roses and the flowers
with the language of their heart... They caress all creatures that they
encounter as if they were friends..."[12]

At the same time, other details that one finds within "Humanity and Its
Responsibilities" are echoed in essays like "An Ideal Society"—not
surprisingly, since the assumption of such responsibilities will lead to the
improvement of society. Thus, turning to the Qur'anic sura 95—"The Fig"
(At-Tin)—where, in verse 4 we read that "we have indeed created man in
the most perfect form and nature" Gülen equates that perfection of form
and nature not only with "the unlimited gifts that [humans] have received,"
but with the notion that "humanity took on the responsibility that the

---

[10] Ibid., 207-8.
[11] Ibid., 208-9.
[12] Fethullah Gülen, "The Horizons of Tranquility," in *Toward a Global Civilization of Love and Tolerance*, (Somerset, NJ: The Light, Inc., 2006), 261-2.

Earth, the sky, and the mountains rejected, in fear that they would not be able to shoulder this responsibility."[13]

The key word is once again responsibility: the vice-regency is not a carte blanche to swallow the world in a self-centered manner—to subject it and have dominion over it simply for our own purposes and selfish needs—but to "develop the gifts with which [we] were adorned and to live according to divine inspiration"[14] as caretakers of each other and of the world around us. Nor is the fulfillment of such responsibilities simple: "Ideal people know that they are being continually tested and refined...."[15]

The other side of caretaking responsibilities is "not [to] bow before anything or anyone other than God... [it is to] resist the seductive attractions of the material world... [it is to] examine all that occurs like a scientist in a laboratory... [and to] dedicate their lives to humanity and [to] leave a much better world for coming generations." [16] Ideal people, genuine humans—those who fulfill the Qur'anic dictum of embracing the perfect form and nature with which God has imbued humans as a concomitant of imbuing us with the responsibilities of vice-regency— "...value all servants of God as being the greatest of people, and appreciate each other as peers."[17]

To seek to arrive at that point is both a desideratum and a fulfillable goal for any and all humans, although "[m]ost of us have not reached this level yet." An ideal society is the one in which we shall have all arrived at that level—such a society is one that converts our everyday world into Eden—and if we have not achieved that goal yet, we are enjoined by Gülen (and commanded by God) to continue to struggle with ourselves and our society to arrive there. This is the real meaning of *jihad*, as Gülen makes clear: the struggle to perfect ourselves and the world, as submitters to God's will that we serve as vice-regents who both appreciate each other as peers and encounter all creatures as friends.

***

Gülen's intellectual resources do not end with the Qur'an or its biblical sibling. As much as he is a teacher of the Qur'an and a careful student of the texts of other religious traditions, his interest also extends to the

---

[13] Fethullah Gülen, "An Ideal Society," in *Toward a Global Civilization of Love and Tolerance*, (Somerset, NJ: The Light, Inc., 2006), 213-4.
[14] Ibid., 214.
[15] Ibid., 214.
[16] Ibid., 216.
[17] Ibid., 216.

beginnings of Western philosophical and scientific thought. At those beginnings stand three figures who tower above all others: Socrates, Plato and Aristotle. For practical purposes in this discussion we may consider Socrates and Plato as one—since as far as we know, Socrates himself wrote nothing down, and in reading his words as reported by Plato[18] we cannot always clearly distinguish between Socrates' own words and ideas as recorded by his star pupil and the words and ideas of Plato himself.

Thus throughout the Platonic corpus one sees the very important distinction between words (*logoi*; sing. = *logos*) and actions (*erga*; sing. = *ergon*). The one presents a theoretical account of what one believes or how one ought to behave under certain circumstances; the other articulates that theoretical account by actualizing it. The distinction between theory and actualization—the interweave between *logos* and *ergon*—is nowhere more emphatically exemplified than in Plato's *Phaedo*.

Set in the prison where Socrates is doomed to die, this dialogue offers the final conversation between the philosopher and his closest friends. In it, Socrates offers a range of different arguments—*logoi*—for why we should understand the soul to be immortal. He argues as to why, therefore, the true philosopher, seeking truths that are difficult to come by in an absolute way while the soul is still "imprisoned" in the ever-demanding body—should embrace death eagerly, as offering an opportunity for the untrammeled soul to seek and find truth.

The outpouring of words along diversely reasoned lines—culminating with a more midrashic account, a *mythos* of how things might be for the soul beyond physical death—is followed by the ultimate *ergon*. Socrates accepts the cup of death-dealing hemlock with great good humor and eagerly quaffs it down, as if it were the finest beverage he had ever tasted. Thus his actions move in perfect counterpoint to his words; his *ergon* echoes his *logos*. His stated eagerness to abandon the body in death to allow his immortal soul to pursue inquiries into truth free of the prison of physical needs is accompanied by action that corroborates that eagerness.

Other Platonic dialogues offer instances of ways in which Socrates acted in a manner unequivocally consistent with the beliefs that he expressed to his friends. We see it in the description of him and his actions (his *erga*) by Alcibiades in the *Symposium*, in the heart of which description Socrates' disdain for death is exemplified in his rescue of the wounded Alcibiades from the battlefield without concern for his own safety. It is Alcibiades' discussion and description that helps us recognize that Socrates' own discussion and description (his own *logos*) regarding

---

[18] And occasionally others, most notably, Xenophon.

love that precedes Alcibiades' arrival to the party really speaks of Socrates himself.

We see the intense relationship between *logos* and *ergon* in the *Crito*, the dialogue that, dramatically speaking, precedes the *Phaedo*—in which a wealthy friend of Socrates wishes to spirit him out of prison and away from his imminent execution. Socrates refuses, noting that, as someone who has championed the laws in Athens his entire adult life, and who has pushed again and again for his fellow citizens to keep cross-examining themselves and their putative understandings of law and justice, he could hardly serve as a model to his children if he fled the prison cell and thus disrespected the laws simply because, in human hands, those laws had led to a death-sentence for him. Thus his *ergon* of remaining in prison to face death affirms the *logos* that he delivers to Crito within the dialogue.

One can recognize a profound emulation of this *logos-ergon* dynamic in Gülen's essay, "The Meaning of Life," at the outset of which, in noting that "[t]he purpose of our creation is obvious: to reach our utmost goals of belief, knowledge, and spirituality; to reflect on the universe, humanity, and God, and thus prove our value as human beings," he goes on to assert: "Thought will provoke action, and thereby start a 'prosperous cycle.'"[19]

The notion of an inherent connection between thought and action for those who truly function as "genuine humans"—as God's vice-regents on earth—is that they "reflect, do what they believe to be right, and then reflect on their behavior."[20] So just as in "Humanity and Its Responsibilities" Gülen articulates an inherent and reciprocal harmony between behaving in a proper way toward the physical universe and directing ourselves (through worship) toward God properly, in this essay behavior and reflection on it offer the possibility of a reciprocal harmony.

Thus when he reiterates the idea that "our duty is to reflect upon our place in life, our responsibilities, and our relationship with this vast universe..." and that "we [who are] the most important living creations in this universe... should reflect upon and observe the universe so that we may realize and fulfill the purpose of our creation,"[21] he attaches such reflection to actions that respect and improve the universe. Our reflection should not have as its goal reflection alone but action that grows out of that reflection. This thought-action matrix is a counterpart to his articulation of the principle of subjecting the universe not merely for our own benefit for the benefit of all the creatures that comprise it.

---

[19] Fethullah Gülen, "The Meaning of Life," in *Toward a Global Civilization of Love and Tolerance*, (Somerset, NJ: The Light, Inc., 2006), 219.
[20] Ibid., 220.
[21] Ibid., 220-1.

Moreover, just as Gülen's own *logoi* prescribe a dynamical balance between thought and action, in the world in which he lives those words have yielded a diversity of actions—*erga*—that are part of the process of improving the world, inspired by his *logoi*. For the movement that is most often referred to by his name—the Gülen Movement—is in fact a movement conceived as one that inherently translates thoughts and words into actions. Its proper name is the *Hizmet* Movement, and the Turkish word *hizmet* means "service. The goal articulated by Gülen in these essays and others is not a goal that is limited to words and reflection. Words are of inevitable importance as instruments for discerning divine interests and intentions, and reflection is important as a basis for such words. But the fulfillment of those intentions and the carrying out of those interests is expressed by the transformation of reflections and words into actions.

Yet another of Gülen's essays—one that is focused on education: "Educational Services are Spreading Throughout the World"—articulates not only why education is so essential to human beings, but what kind of education best suits us as a species. Thus, "[h]umans are creatures composed not only of a body and a mind, or feelings and a spirit; rather we are harmonious compositions of all these elements... [e]ach person is a creature made up of feelings that cannot be satisfied by the mind, and a creature of spirit; it is through the spirit that we acquire our essential human identity."[22] Thus he emphasizes the threefold nature of the human being and the importance of educational systems that engage all three components of that nature: the physical, the intellectual and the emotional/ spiritual.

Moreover, he speaks yet again in this particular essay of the importance of the physical universe: the world around us, of which we are a part, is equated with no less an entity than the Qur'an. Both God's word spoken through the prophet Muhammad and the physical universe must be studied and reflected upon, for both have the potential to teach us about God and what God's expectations of us are. "[T]he universe is just a large Qur'an that has been physically created by God for our instruction."[23] The world is likened to the text in which we are referred to as a vice-regent with responsibility for the world, just as we may understand human responsibility to encompass studying, reflecting on, and speaking and acting out of the instruction of the Qur'an.

---

[22] Fethullah Gülen, "Educational Services Are Spreading Throughout the World," in *Toward a Global Civilization of Love and Tolerance*, (Somerset, NJ: The Light, Inc., 2006), 309.
[23] Ibid., 312.

Gülen underscores the importance of the sciences as part of our educational systems—not in opposition to but in harmony with spirituality. And as he observes that "nature is much more than a heap of material or an accumulation of objects: it has a certain sacredness, for it is an arena in which God's Beautiful Names are displayed,"[24] he reiterates from the angle of evolving an effective system of education the notion that "having dominion" over the earth, "subjecting" it and being "God's vice-regent" over it is not a matter of treating it as a pile of goods for our gratification, but as a sacred expression of God's creative power and presence with which we want (or should want) a strong connection.

Gülen observes not only in broad terms that "[r]eligion guides sciences, determines their real goal, and puts moral and universal human values before sciences as guides," but that a misreading of God's intentions—or an abandoning of reflection upon them—can lead and has led not only to "the wars and revolutions of the twentieth century that killed hundreds of millions of people…" but to the problem "…of environmental pollution, which has been caused by scientific materialism …,"[25] which problem humans who function correctly as vice-regents are obligated to try to solve.

But the point is that all of these *logoi* directed to shaping an educational system that will train our children to be conscious of such a tapestry of interwoven issues are reflected in the *hizmet* movement which bears Gülen's imprint. This last-referenced essay ("Educational Services …") is not merely a prescription of what we need as a forward-moving species, but a description, as its title implies, of what is already evolving under the auspices of *hizmet* as an instrument to *spread* the idea of *hizmet* in a wider circle.

Thus we may note that, since 1991, several hundred schools sponsored or inspired by the Gülen Movement, at all educational levels, have opened not only in Turkey, but in the Turkic nations of south central Asia, various post-Soviet states, such as Moldavia, Ukraine and Georgia, as well as in western countries such as Australia, Canada, France, Germany, and the United States. Perhaps most recently, the Nigerian Turkish Nile University opened its doors in Abuja, Nigeria on December 9, 2009.

More to the point of our discussion, from the elementary to the university level, thousands of students, across national, ethnic and religious boundaries study an extended array of disciplines: science, mathematics, history, language, literature, social and cultural studies, art, music and

---

[24] Ibid., 313.
[25] Ibid., 312-13.

sports. The curriculum at all levels is designed to consider the intellectual and emotional development of students, as well as their physical development.[26]

From Turkey itself to Central Asia, Europe and Africa to America, Gülen Movement students are provided with teachers of exemplary dedication, curricula of ambitious quality—and an embracing vision that looks to global betterment through the teaching of tolerance of difference and the embrace of dialogue.[27] It is most often the case, as time moves on, that former students become teachers in these schools, and their interest and commitment—their dedication to promoting the encompassing principles espoused by the *Hizmet* Movement—are palpable. They teach, in fact, by example: their *logoi* are consistently demonstrated by *erga*. By this I mean both that they live lives consistent with what they teach and that, at a basic level, their devotion to their teaching is measurable by their willingness to put in more than the "ordinary" hours to help their students grow.

Thus both those who teach and those who study in the Gülen Movement schools are in the process of embracing and expressing and/or learning to embrace a three-fold (intellectual, spiritual/emotional, physical) mode of engaging each other and the world. They embrace the importance of *hizmet* as a centerpiece in that engagement, the point and purpose of which is to become leaders who help improve the world—to have dominion and be divinely ordained vice-regents in the sense addressed in the various essays by Gülen to which this discussion of his thinking has referred.[28]

---

[26] Thus for instance, Fatih University outside Istanbul includes Faculties of Engineering, Economics and Administrative Sciences, Law, Medicine, Arts and Sciences as well as Vocational Training; within the arts and Sciences, available departments in six different language and literature concentrations as well as departments that range from Biology and Chemistry to Psychology and Sociology. There is a wide array of cultural and sports activities, and 71 student clubs and groups, with a strong emphasis on multi-culturalism.

[27] I am asserting this based not only on book-research, but on the experience of having visited a number of Gülen Movement schools in August, 2009 and having had the opportunity to speak with administrators, teachers and students at several different grade levels.

[28] Gülen's vision, interestingly, extends beyond Plato with respect to an ideal education system. Plato would eliminate subjects in the arts that, for various reasons were deemed detrimental to the training of his leaders, the Guardians. Thus passages in the *Iliad*, for instance, that represent Achilles as a cry-baby after having been insulted by Agamemnon (discussed in *Republic* 387e8-388d1); or the visual arts, which, he believed, offered mere imitation of reality—which is itself

Thus we may observe the meeting between Socratic/Platonic *logos* and *ergon* not only in the writing of Gülen and the ideas that he champions in his essays, but in the activation of those ideas in a myriad of ways, of which the Gülen educational system and its ties to these ideas—as a promoter of *hizmet*—is, for the purposes of our discussion, most noteworthy.

Moreover, both the words of Fetulleh Gülen and the actions that those words inspire may also be seen to emulate and have as a goal the achievement of what Plato's most important disciple, Aristotle, articulated in his use of the Greek word *harmonia*. *Harmonia* is the bringing of apparently opposed ideas into dynamic synthesis. The primary context of the term, thanks to the early Hellenistic writer, Aristoxenus, and thus as it is used in English and other languages, is music, where "harmony" may be understood as the coming together of two musical tones in a manner that offers a phonic synthesis that is pleasing to the ear. Gülen's entire approach to the world as expressed in his essays and as activated in the schools that claim inspiration from the movement that bears his name bespeaks *harmonia* as a goal. We see that he himself uses the concept of harmony repeatedly—musical metaphors are among his favorites—in his discussions (*logoi*) and we may observe the activation (*erga*) of that *harmonia* in the Gülen schools.

Moreover, the *harmonia* that he offers, specifically, between religion and science, in both the *logoi* of those essays and the *erga* of those schools, suggests a strongly Aristotelian—albeit in *harmonia* with a Platonic—approach to truth. Thus Plato emphasized that ultimate and perfect truth regarding the Good and its concomitants exists only in a reality other than our own—the reality of the Forms/Ideas, that exists *beyond* our reality, of which ours is only a *mimesis*, an imitation. But Aristotle's expansion of the fields of Platonic thought to encompass the natural sciences reflects his conviction that astute observation of the world around us, in partnership with our analytical minds, can yield absolute and ultimate truths.

---

merely an imitation of the "Forms"/"Ideas" (*Republic* 596b1-598c2)—would not be part of his curriculum. But the Gülen educational system emphatically includes the arts, which are recognized as an essential part of shaping a multi-dimensional human being. Even poetry or prose that offers unheroic-behaving heroes can help the student to consider what it is that *makes* a human being heroic—what it is that makes a genuine, ideal human being; and visual art doesn't *imitate* reality but *re-visions and transforms* it through the mind of the artist, creating something with its own validity and not merely offering a pale reflection of objective reality.

Gülen's thinking represents an Aristotelian *harmonia* between Platonic and Aristotelian thinking as that thinking is applicable to the discussions in Genesis and the Qur'an. In Gülen's writing the deep awareness of the Divine Reality beyond our own is synthesized to the conviction that our vice-regency of the world which we are enjoined to subject and over which we are commanded to have dominion, obligates us to care for it. Gülen emphasizes the importance of investigative science, and the analysis of the physical world with intellectual reasoning. Yet he both believes in an emotional/spiritual reality that transcends the physical/intellectual reality in which we humans dwell, and argues that the latter is a result of the former: the creation, including ourselves, was shaped by a Creator who continues to be interested in and involved with us.

His repeated articulation of the principle that, as a species, we need to apply the meeting point among the physical, intellectual and spiritual to our stewardship of—our vice-regency over—the earth applies directly to the shaping of ideas and indeed policies and actions that offer eco-justice as part of their foundation. Gülen's thought suggests that the act of caring for the world in a genuine way—developing our understanding of it as we develop its potential—offers a means of more affectively establishing a oneness with the Divine Reality that is the author of our own reality, which oneness is the ultimate goal of all three Abrahamic traditions.

"SELF AND OTHERS" FOR RELIGIOUS ECOLOGY: AN ANALYSIS OF GÜLEN'S THOUGHT

HEON KIM

In this chapter, I survey Gülen's thought in line with religious ecology and within frameworks of the concept of self and others. Each of these terms, 'religious ecology' and 'self and others,' has resonance in diverse academic fields. Yet, there is a significant lack of research of both in conjunction. By using the concept of 'self and others' as a framework for religious ecology, this chapter analyzes Gülen's thought of the relationships of 'God, human and nature' and the current ecological crisis.

I present, first, 'the separation thesis between self and others,' and carefully draw from it a paradigmatic root of the ecological crisis. Paralleling the separation thesis, I then examine Gülen's idea of ecology from the frameworks of self-others identities and relationships. I revisit and extend my previous works on Gülen's ideal of "humanity in dialogue" that views humanity as an interdependent unity of self and other and as an object of love, tolerance and dialogue. I considered this view to be an alternative to the popular presumption of 'the autonomously privileged self over others' and 'the antagonistic self-other.' Proceeding from this, this present study directly delves into Gülen's idea of ecology, and demonstrates that 'self and others' in his thought concerns 'nature and humanity' and 'Nature-human relationship.' Accordingly, this chapter suggests an ontological/theological basis and considerable moral principles of the nature-human relationship for a discussion about peace in and with the world.

The Separation Thesis between Self and Others

The idea of self and others is quite modern,[1] although its origin arguably dates back to the ancient dualistic worldview. In today's world – especially in the West, the idea has become widely employed in diverse academic areas as well as public discourse within the purview of many new-*isms*, including colonialism, modernism, capitalism, social constructionism, postcuturalism, postmodernism, neo-liberalism and globalism. A multidisciplinary conceptualization and contexualization of self-others and the relationship has greatly helped reconsider human nature, existence, experience and phenomena in history, culture, society, economics and politics.

An underlying premise in this wide usage is that a self exists with others and defines itself in terms of others. In some detail, a self - understood as an individual, the word which originated from Latin *individuus* that means 'not (*in*) divisible (*dividuus*)' to denote a being that can no longer be "divided" - is separate from others, and thereby forms relationship with others who are intrinsically and dialectically opposed to the self. As Adrian Carr notes, "this view has been termed the separation thesis," which "is pervasive in Western thinking," as "western thought is imbued with a style of thinking based on dichotomy and binary opposition, like right/wrong, rational/emotional, nature/nurture, public/private, and so forth."[2]

The dichotomy and binary opposition between self and others is linked to another assumption that 'self is necessarily *prior to* other' and "in the intersubjective system of self and other, self must necessarily be privileged over other."[3] Out of the prioritized and privileged self over others comes a struggle for predominance of self over others, and the predominance of self brings about conflicts with others. Therefore, the relationships between self and others become not simply opposing but conflicting.

The separation thesis between self and others in this premise has been employed in diverse areas to identify problems facing humanity. Philosophers engaged in ontological questions, like if others exist differently from self or if a self differentiates others to construct its own identity. Anthropologists as well as sociologists examined how groups

---

[1] See Charles Taylor, "The Dialogical Self," in *Rethinking Knowledge: Reflections Across the Disciplines*, Robert F. Goodman and Walter R. Fisher, eds. (Albany: SUNY Press, 1995), 57.
[2] Adrian Carr, "The 'separation thesis' of self and other: metatheorizing a dialectic alternative," *Theory & Psychology* 13:1 (2003): 117.
[3] Ibid.

defined as "us" exclude others (them). While psychologists analyzed in what mechanism the space between self and others invoke a psychical process of an individual's reaction, economists attempted to figure out to what degree the opposing relationship between self and others alienates each other around material sources and gains. The self-other relationship also attracted historians to examine how the relationship has caused subordination of a self to others or vice versa. In a more recent context, diverse answers were suggested to the question whether the relationship is imperative to raise peculiar *isms* (like nationalism and fundamentalism) in globalism. As an example, Michel Foucault's post-structural reading of history of self-other relationship in power-domination[4] and Edward Said's innovative concept of 'Orientalist Others' to explain a justification of colonialization and 'civilization'[5] are well-circulated. Likewise, many scholarly works have been produced, not only by utilizing, but also to identify the separation thesis. What is now apparent is the separation thesis with an emphasis on the opposing and conflicting relationship between self and others. The thesis, as prevalent in human history, especially in the western worldview, has been attributed to a paradigmatic cause of inferioritization, alienation and demonization of others, and of justification of self to dominate, colonize, civilize, develop and exploit others. Along this line, Calvin Schrag's recent examination on "how does that which is other become evil" considers the concept of others and otherness as a source of evil today.[6]

I traced back what separates between self and others to form the binary conflict opposition between them. In my analysis, ideology, materialism and religion are the three sources that most frequently (re) appear in contemporary trends. As I examined elsewhere,[7] a view of dialectic

---

[4] See Michel Foucault, *The Government of Self and Others: Lectures at the Collège de France 1982-1983,* ed. Arnold I. Davidson, trans. Graham Burchell (New York: Palgrave Macmillan, 2010).
[5] Edward Said, *Orientalism* (New York: Pantheon Books, 1978).
[6] Calvin O. Schrag, "Otherness and the Problem of Evil: How Does That Which is Other Become Evil?," *International Journal for Philosophy of Religion* 60: 1/3 (Dec. 2006): 156.
[7] Heon Kim, "Dialogic Humanism: Gülen's Alternative to Dialectic Humanity." (paper presented at a symposium on *Preventing Violence and Achieving World Peace,* University of Maryland, College Park, MD, October 2009) and Heon Kim, "Gülen's Dialogic Sufism: A Constructional and Constructive Factor of Dialogue," (paper presented at Islam in the Age of Global Challenges: Alternative Perspectives of the Gülen Movement, Georgetown University, Washington, D.C., November, 2008). Available online at
www.gulenconference.net/files/Georgetown/2008_HeonKim.pdf

tension or opposition between self and others evolved from "the ideologically superior self and inferior others" in the dialectic philosophy of Friedrich Hegel (d. 1831), "the politico-economically alienated self-others" in the materialistic worldview of Karl Marx (d. 1883), and "the religiously incompatible self-others" in the view of Samuel Huntington (d. 2008). I have coined this view a "dialectical approach to humanity," which presupposes an opposing and conflicting relationship between self and others, and causes a theoretical/phenomenological gap among civilizations, nations, social classes and humanity itself.

I find in this dialectical approach to humanity a considerable clue for the intellectual background of human domination over nature and the ecological crisis. Though it was not until recent times that we came to be well aware of, humanity's perception of nature as the independent other has a much deeper, wider and older history than our exclusive treatment of other human beings. Be it indifference, unconcern or insensibility, the exclusivist way we have viewed and treated nature came to be taken for granted for a long time and has sedimented in our collective (un)consciousness. As such, to dig up these sediments is not an easy task, which may require a massive, perhaps revolutionary, change of our thought. It is however an imminent task to comprehend the reasons behind the contemporary ecological crisis. Regardless of the fact that the notion of self and others has served as a key to deconstruct our human problems in almost all aspects, there is a quite limited number of research that analyzes our ecological problems within the frameworks of 'self and others.'

That being said, the following three works are remarkable. First, Carolyn Merchant's path-breaking *The Death of Nature* unfolds a compact history of the western approach to nature. This now well-known work attempts to answer how "nature came to be viewed as a resource to be subjected to control with human beings as her earthly managers."[8] In Merchant's analysis, "the removal of animistic, organic assumptions about the cosmos constituted the death of nature – the most far reaching effect of the scientific revolution. Because nature was now viewed as a system of dead, inert particles moved by external, rather than inherent forces, the mechanical framework itself could legitimate the manipulation of nature."[9] With a focus on Francis Bacon's (d. 1626) doctrine of human domination over nature, Merchant also illustrates how literalist Christian belief in the Fall of Adam and Eve from God's grace in the Garden of Eden worked together with the Scientific revolution of the sixteenth and the seventeenth

---

[8] Carolyn Merchant, *The Death of Nature: Women, Ecology, and the Scientific Revolution* (San Francisco: Harper & Row, 1980), 205.
[9] Ibid., 193.

centuries to create a mechanical and mechanistic paradigm of human separation from and dominion over nature. She goes further arguing that this mechanical paradigm "had associated with it a framework of values based on power, fully compatible with the directions taken by commercial capitalism."[10]

To a certain degree, this analysis enforces my proposed dialectic approach to humanity. It observes a powerful combination of the three elements, ideology, materialism and religion, which have inclusively acted to be a source of not only human separation from other humans but also human domination over nature. I further read the ideological and theological separation between self and others (corresponding to humanity and nature), and see it as a cause of a mechanical approach to nature. This mechanistically radical separation continues to be dominant, being instrumentalized in capitalist and neo-liberalist discourse to form a mechanistic worldview.

More recently, Gilbert LaFreniere brings further Merchant's analysis. His work *The Decline of Nature* assumes that there is "the fundamental layer or structure responsible for human abuse of nature."[11] LaFreniere finds the layer in "unconscious, subliminal destructive attitudes toward nature" that "permeate the Western mind, and especially the American mind."[12] He points out, first, the Judeo-Christian ideal of dominion over nature with a theological slogan of "turning wilderness into a garden" – especially, the Christian who "has essentially used up the natural resources of western Europe under a worldview which explained humanity as God's favorite creature inhabiting Earth, designed for humanity, at the center of the cosmos."[13] The modern period has stiffened this Western worldview, "leading toward peculiarly Western destructiveness towards nature, overlaid upon the natural utilitarian and Christian dominion components."[14] The Scientific Revolution, modern science, technologies and commercial capitalism followed to integrate "the model of a perfect, God-designed mechanical cosmos, the key to more masterful manipulation of nature."[15] Along this line of ecological deconstruction of the history, LaFreniere reads "modernity" as "a set of ideas, values, and beliefs," which is overlaid upon older Christian ideas of dominion over and stewardship of

---

[10] Ibid.
[11] Gilbert LaFreniere, *The Decline of Nature*: *Environmental History and the Western Worldview*. (Bethesda, MD : Academica Press, 2008), 341.
[12] Ibid.
[13] Ibid., 345.
[14] Ibid.
[15] Ibid.

nature.[16] Concurring with Oswald Spengler's *Decline of the West* that portrays "the history of a steadily increasing, fateful fight between man's world and the universe," LaFreniere asserts that "This human tragedy inevitably grows out of the human struggle with nature, and the outcome is the defeat of every higher culture, of every civilization in the long run… in Man and Technics it is the result of the universal struggle between humankind and nature."[17]

LaFreniere's *The Decline of Nature*, just as Merchant's *The Death of Nature*, strongly implies that at the bottom line of the ecological problems lies the separation thesis. Particularly, the underlined terms of "the universal struggle and fight between humanity and nature" make salient the conflicting and dialectic relationship between self and others.

A number of the ecological studies have been also made by Islamic ecologists, some of whom concur with *The Decline of Nature* and *The Death of Nature*. Seyyid Hossein Nasr, the foremost Muslim ecologist, gives a representative voice. He articulates that "the destruction of the environment is the result of the modern attempt to view the natural environment as an ontologically independent order of reality."[18] More specifically, Nasr attributes the destruction to the western civilization, which since the advent of Renaissance humanism "has absolutized earthly man."[19] He goes on arguing that "while depriving man of a center and creating a veritable centerless culture and art, Western humanism has sought to bestow upon this centerless humanity the quality of absoluteness. It is this purely earthly man defined by rationalism and humanism who developed seventeenth-century science based upon the domination and conquest of nature, who sees nature as an enemy, and who continues to plunder and destroy the natural environment always in the name of the rights of man, which are seen as absolute."[20] This argument can be read as that the human-centric (self-centric) view of nature (other) as "the ontologically independent reality" leads to the view of nature as an "enemy," and thereby, in a reminiscence of Karl Marx's notion of alienation in capitalism, invoking "alienation from nature" and embedding it "in the secularized Western psyche and mind."[21] This aspect turns us

---

[16] Ibid., 344.
[17] Ibid., 393.
[18] Seyyed Hossein Nasr, "Islam and the Environmental Crisis," in *Spirit and Nature,* eds. Steven C. Rockefeller and John C. Elder, (Boston: Beacon Press, 1992), 89.
[19] Ibid., 94.
[20] Ibid., 94-95.
[21] Ibid., 102.

back to the separation thesis and the dialectical approach, suggesting the latter as the basis of the former.

The separation thesis between self and others as implicitly underlined in the represented three ecological studies leads us to interrogate if we see nature as others, in a more nuanced term, if we *otherize* nature - not as an organic part of us but as a mechanical other. In this account, the separation thesis provides a considerable frame for an in-depth understanding of the environmental issues and the ecological crisis. As a case study, I now turn to analyze Gülen's idea of Eco-Justice and ecology from this framework.

Self and Others in Gülen's Thought

Quite contrary to the separation thesis, Gülen's thought accentuates that self and others exist, of necessity, mutually constituted without any privileged identity and opposing relationship.

To begin with, Gülen has shown a deep concern on the problems facing contemporary humanity, as:

> Today, people are talking about many things: the danger of war and frequent clashes all over the world, water and air pollution, hunger, the increasing erosion of moral values, and so on. As a result, many other concerns have come to the fore: peace, contentment, ecology, justice, tolerance, and dialogue. Unfortunately, those who should be tackling these problems tend to do so by seeking further ways to conquer and control nature and produce more lethal weapons.[22]

In direct regard to Eco-Justice in society and environment, he further points out that "only a few people seem to realize that social harmony and peace with nature, between people, and within the individual only can come about when the material and spiritual realms are reconciled."[23] In his part, "Peace with nature, peace and justice in society, and personal integrity are possible when one is at peace with Heaven."[24] In this context, Gülen regards religion as the source for an alternative solution to the ecological crisis. He is convinced:

> Religion reconciles opposites that seem to be mutually exclusive: religion–science, this world–the next world, nature–Divine Books, the material–the spiritual, and spirit–body. Religion can erect a defense against the

---

[22] Gülen, "The Necessity of Interfaith Dialogue: A Muslim Perspective," *The Fountain*, 3: 31 (2000): 4.
[23] Ibid.
[24] Ibid.

destruction caused by scientific materialism, put science in its proper place, and end long-standing conflicts among nations and peoples. The natural sciences, which should act as steps of light leading people to God, have become a cause of unbelief on a previously unknown scale.[25]

This conviction revisits our topic of 'self and others.' As opposed to the separation thesis, Gülen sees religion not as a source of conflict between self and others but as a source of reconciliation between them. What he means by religion here is arguably Islam, but corresponding to his most-well known and distinctive advocate of dialogue between religions, it more accurately refers to an inclusive Islam not an exclusivist Islam between Islam (self) and other religions (others). At this point, just as I attempted earlier to present the relationship between self and others at the center of ecological discourse, I also find it at the core of Gülen's thought of ecology and eco-justice.

In detail, Gülen does not oppose to the notion of the fragmented self from others. But he clearly rejects the dialectically opposing and conflicting relationship between self and others. Above all, in his theological worldview, all human beings are equal, and there is no such concept of the privileged self over others. Gülen considers human beings as "mirrors of the names, attributes, and deeds of God."[26] This implies that God is the Other in term of human-self - not a simple any-other but the capitalized Other, in a reminiscence of Emmanuel Levinas' concept of "The Infinite Other" who exists "not simply the first other but other than the other"[27] and to whom a self encounters and is thereby ultimately realized. To this extent, Gülen's consideration of humanity as the mirror of God does not oppose to "the mirror of the other" as stated earlier in the separation thesis. However, Gülen holds quite differently. Unlike the privileged place of self in the separation thesis, human beings as the mirrors of God condition the equality of all human beings in terms of divinity. As Gülen reasons, God's Mercy and Love are indiscriminative in allowing every human being equally to reflect His Manifestations, and therefore, all human beings, irrespective of differences of religions, races, wealth and social status, are equal in the capacity and capability of

---

[25] Ibid.

[26] Gülen, *The Statue of Our Souls: Revival in Islamic Thought and Activism* (New Jersey: The Light Inc., 2005), 112.

[27] Emmanuel Levinas, *God, Death, and Time* (Stanford, CA: Stanford University Press, 2000), 224. Arguably Gülen's idea of "the Infinite Other" is different from not only Levinas' but also Derrida's "the Wholly Other." However, in the line of the mono-theistic theology can a basic agreement be found. As for the differences, a further separate research will be worthy.

mirroring Divine Light. Moreover, contrary to the separation thesis that connects self and others with enmity and conflict, Gülen argues that human individuals relate to each other with love, assuming that the foremost of the human reflections of divine names and attributes is love. He states that "a human lives with love, is made happy by love and makes those around him or her happy with love. In the vocabulary of humanity, love is life; we feel and sense each other with love. God Almighty has not created a stronger relation than love, this chain that binds humans one to another."[28] Further, in this love-centric theology, while the dialectical approach instrumentalizes ideology, materialism and/or religion to construct the opposing and conflicting relationship between self and others, love deconstructs the opposites to make the opposites reconciling and return their opposing relationship to harmony.

It is through the love-centric worldview that Gülen also considers nature. He says that "Above all else, just as God wove the universe like lace on the loom of love, the most magical and charming music in the bosom of existence is always love... Universal love shows itself throughout the cosmos in the fact that each particle helps and supports every other particle. This is true to such an extent that the most dominant factor in the spirit of existence is love."[29] Thus, to Gülen, love is the most essential element in every being/thing in the universe, and therefore, "the Earth is nothing but a ruin without love to keep it fresh and alive... In this over-polluted world, where evil is everywhere, if there is something that has been left untouched and clean, that is love."[30]

On this basis and through his numerous writings, sermons and media interviews, Gülen has developed a highly sophisticated theological schema regarding 'God, human and nature relationship.' Considering the allowed space of this essay, I illustrate the schema from the following figure, which focuses on the self-other relationship.

First of all, all four circles in this figure are interconnected with love to illustrate Gülen's love-centric worldview. This love-binding connection does not see the separation between self and others *per se* as the root cause of human problems in general and the ecological crisis in particular. Truly the self here has an autonomous identity, which is yet connected with others not by enmity but by love that keeps coexistence and cooperation realized.

---

[28] Gülen, *Toward a Global Civization of Love and Tolerance*, 7.
[29] Ibid., 4.
[30] Ibid., 7.

GOD, HUMANS AND NATURE

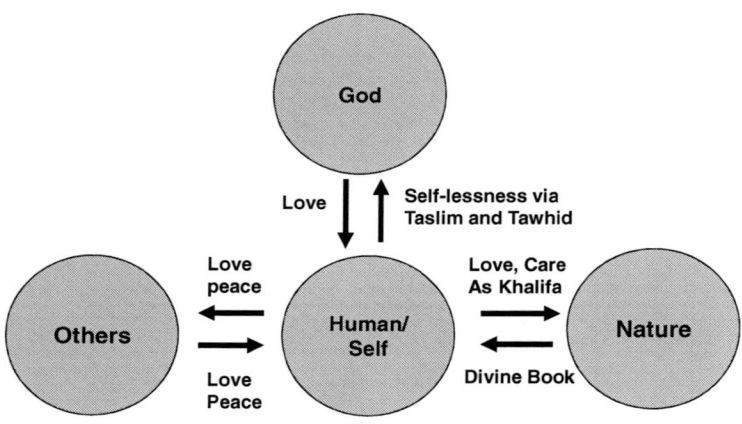

In a sense, this autonomous identity invokes Jacques Derrida's notion of *difference*. According to Derrida, all identities involve their differences and relations with respect to outside of the object: due to this relational independence, an identity is not to erase other identities, which are indispensable for the historical, social, and geographical production of new meaning. This understanding influenced in a current academic discourse on interfaith dialogue to address the wounds of irreconcilable differences and to promote ecumenical and mutual understanding of different faiths. In my reading of both Derrida's *difference* and its related discourse, the difference actually infers differentiation, which comes from categorization and discrimination between self and others based upon, for instance, ideology (Hegel), materialism (Marx) and/or religion (Huntington). In other words, differentiation appears when a self considers his/her identity predominant over others' identities, i.e., the identification of superiority over inferiority. Similarly, in Gülen's schema, the root of conflict lies not in the different entities themselves, but in a 'self.' More precisely, he considers egoistic carnal-self (*nafs*) to be the source of the self's privileged differentiation and distinction from others – the primary source that brings human vices and weakness by constantly blemishing the divinely endowed polished mirror of humanity and consequently decentralizing love in her relationship with others.

In Gülen's theology, self can be best purified and polished through spiritual practices, and the best way - if not the only way - for the spiritual practices can be found in the tradition of Sufism that has been proved by great Sufi spiritual saints with a millennium-long history.

In this context, Gülen approves Sufism as Islamic spirituality and presents great Sufi saints like Jalal al-Din Rumi (d. 1273) and Yunus Emre (d. 1321) as role-models. As I extensively examined elsewhere,[31] Sufism locates at the foundation of Gülen's life, thought and teachings. Love in God, humans and nature relationship is likewise conceptualized within the purview of Sufism and Sufic humanism. Pertinent to today's world of materialism, Gülen accentuates Sufism as a "principle that leads a human being to be nonexistent by comprehending his/her impotence, poverty and nothingness, and by dissolving him/herself before the attributes of the existence of the Truth that forms the essence of the created."[32] On this basis and directly addressing to the contemporary materialized and caplitalized humanity who is identified with economic ability and power (*homo economicus*), he proposes a spiritual path toward and on self's awareness of 'impotence, poverty and nothingness.'

To follow Gülen's rationale, self's awareness and wakefulness of impotence, poverty and nothingness before God lets one become completely dependent on and absolute surrender to Him. This is called in Islamic theology *taslim*, absolute submission and surrender to God, One Absolute (*al-Mutlak*) and One Rich (*al-Ghani*). By means of *taslim*, the part/self/humanity becomes reconciled to the Whole and to the Universe. This is what *tawhid* or Unity refers to. In particular, in Sufi terms and tradition, it denotes self's annihilation in God, and in Gülen's thought, selflessness and nothingness in terms of God.

In this sense, I named the vertical line from human/self to God in the above figure 'Self-lessness via Taslim and Tawhid.' This line is interacted with God's Love down to human/self. As a natural consequence, it leads self toward love of "others" in her horizontal relationship. Gülen is convinced that when one reduces gradually feelings arising from self-love of the carnal self in relation to other beings/things, s/he "is to be loving and tolerant toward everyone, to see the universe as a cradle of brotherhood/sisterhood."[33] In the process, love dilutes the differentiation

---

[31] My unpublished doctoral dissertation is the first extensive research on Sufism in Gülen's thought and the Gülen movement. See Heon Kim, "The Nature and Role of Sufism in Contemporary Islam: A Case Study of the Life, Thought and Teachings of Fethullah Gülen" (PhD diss., Temple University, 2008).

[32] Gülen, *Emerald Hills of the Heart: Key Concepts in the Practice of Sufism 2* (New Jersey: Light, 2004), 257.

[33] Ibid., 263.

between self and other constructed by egoistic carnal self, and in the long run, realizes peace (*Islam*) in self's horizontal relationship with others.

Others in this context is not limited to other human beings, but includes nature. Just as self gives and takes others with love and peace, self/humanity sees nature as an object of love and care. Since the term of 'care' may be misunderstood in a negative connotation to denote a human-centered arrogant approach to Nature, it is necessary to note Gülen's perception of Nature, prior to understanding of his view of the Nature-human relationship.

Gülen is clear in defining nature as a divine book. He appreciates:

> Nature is, in its particulars and as a whole, an exhibition of Divine miracles. However, rather than call it an exhibition, we prefer to call it a 'book'. For we sense and study it as a book and observe it in admiration as if looking through a book gilded in a very splendid way. Appearing before us every morning arrayed in a new, dazzling and richly decorated dress, it breathes into us a new life and spirit and enraptures us.[34]

Nature is a divine source, which God encompasses and His *Tawhid* manifests throughout. Gülen adds that "God attends or shows attention for the universe and whatever is in it from the perspective of His Grace, Majesty, and Perfection, which demonstrates His absolute freedom from any defects or from having partners. This attention is called "the all-encompassing attention," [and] This all-encompassing attention is also described as "the manifestation of Unity" - the overall manifestation of His Names throughout the universe."[35]

Thereby, Gülen reasons:

> Whatever has been created has a purpose. Take the example of ecology. Everything, no matter how apparently insignificant, has a significant role and purpose... Nothing is in vain; rather, every item, activity, and event has many purposes... Everything that exists, and the universe as a whole, display a magnificent harmony and order in themselves and in their interrelationships... All things in the universe, regardless of distance, help each other. This mutual helping is so comprehensive that, for example, almost all things, among them air and water, fire and soil, the sun and the sky, help us in an extraordinarily prearranged manner. Our bodily cells,

---

[34] Gülen, "The Nature We Have Destroyed," *The Fountain* 15 (July – September, 1996). The entire text is available online. Accessed November 10, 2010, http://www.fountainmagazine.com/article.php?ARTICLEID=344.

[35] Gülen, "Nazar and Tawajjuh (Attention and Regard)," accessed November 10, 2010, http://en.fgulen.com/key-concepts-in-the-practice-of-sufism/3193-attention-and-regard.html.

members, and systems work together to keep us alive. Soil and air, water
and heat, and bacteria cooperate with each other to benefit plants.[36]

Thus, "All life is a symphony of mutual helping and love," in conformity
with our discussion here, between self and others.

Gülen holds that in this world of mutual love and support, the duty of
humanity is to love and care nature to preserve it as a divine book. In this
regard, and to the extent of his love-centric worldview, Gülen is convinced
that "without misusing the love in their spirit and for the sake of the love
in their own nature, every person should offer real help and support to
others. They should protect the general harmony that has been put in the
spirit of existence, considering both the natural laws and the laws that have
been made to govern human life."[37]

This idea echoes the Qur'anic concept of *khalifa*, the key term for
Islamic ecology. *Khalifa* means vice-gerent, and the Qur'an records
human being as God's *khalifa* on the earth, as it asserts that "I am setting
on the earth a vice-gerent"[38] This quality of vice-gerent is, however, often
misinterpreted as the divine sanction of humanity to use nature freely and
the justification of human exploitation of the environment. Sayyed
Husseyin Nasr challenges this view by interpreting that "in the same way
that God sustains and cares for the world, humankind as His vice-gerent
must nurture and care for the ambience in which they play the central role.
They cannot neglect the care of the natural world without betraying that
"trust" (*al-amanah*) which they accepted when they bore witness to God's
lordship in the pre-eternal covenant (*al-mithag*)..."[39]

In his interpretation of human identity as God's *khalifa* on the earth,
Gülen puts forth human responsibility to "love and care" for nature, as
illustrated in the above figure. In particular, he sees people of faith as:

> Their faith in God and the characteristics of their faith open up the
> possibility of acquainting themselves with everything, and thus they see all
> existence—living or not—as a family. They make contact with the rest of
> creation, taking an active part in the life of things and in their conscience
> they feel the vastness of the title of vicegerent which has been bequeathed
> to them... They evaluate existence in a way that in no way resembles
> materialist and naturalist depictions, but with the eye of a person of faith
> who associates everything with God, and in response, they receive

---

[36] Gülen, *The Essentials of Islamic Faith* (New Jersey: The Light Inc, 2006), 5-6.
[37] Gülen, *Toward a Global Civization of Love and Tolerance*, 7.
[38] 2:30
[39] Nasr, "Islam and the Environmental Crisis," in *Spirit and Nature,* eds. Steven C.
Rockefeller and John C. Elder (Boston: Beacon Press, 1992), 92.

recognition from all that is around them. They receive messages of confidence from all the things with which they come into contact and respond with an attitude expressing the same confidence. They are not afraid of anyone and do not cause anyone to fear; they embrace all as their brethren. They shower smiles upon all things; they sip water, breath air and accept all manners of presents as blessings from God. They inhale the scent of the Earth and those that it gives birth to as if it were the sweetest of aromas. They salute the orchards and gardens, the mountains and valleys, the grasses and trees, the roses and the flowers with the language of their heart, as if these things too had senses. They caress all creatures that they encounter as if they were friends assigned to keep them company in this guesthouse. With every action they demonstrate that they have been sent to the Earth as a sign for agreement and reconciliation.[40]

If we do not put this duty of vice-gerent into works, Gülen warns that it "results in a very severe punishment." He further confirms that "If we allow ourselves to be dominated by our evil-commanding selves and not our hearts (which must overflow with knowledge and love of the Creator), we are destined to become fuel for the fires of Hell."[41]

The ecological crisis that we face today then means to Gülen that we must have allowed our evil-commanding selves to dominate us and thereby exploit nature. In fact, he laments in many passages, for instance:

What a pity it is that this magnificent book, this charming exhibition, which the infinitely Merciful One has created and presented to man to observe and study and to be exhilarated by, is no longer given any more care than is given to a heap of junk or rubbish. Worse than that, it is more and more becoming a wasteland and like a dunghill... And earth, that treasure of Divine grace and munificence, is a wilderness no longer productive and a ruin without any ecological balance. Like everything else entrusted to us, we have deplorably treated this 'book', this magnificent exhibition, which is an embodiment of Divine grace and mercy. How deplorably and awkwardly we have treated plains and residential places, which we have changed into deserts and heaps of ruin. How deplorably and gracelessly we have treated seas and rivers, which we have polluted. Again, how deplorably and awkwardly we have treated air and water, and fields, forests, and gardens, which we have made unfavourable to any life.[42]

---

[40] Gülen, *Toward a Global Civization of Love and Tolerance*, 161-162.
[41] Gülen, *The Essentials of the Islamic Faith*, 122.
[42] Gülen, "The Nature We Have Destroyed," *The Fountain* 15 (July - September 1996).

To Gülen, this destruction of nature/other results in nothing but self-destruction. In his words, "truly, by changing this Paradise-like world to a hell, how deplorably and awkwardly we have treated ourselves! Unless we improve this world, whose order we have destroyed and which we have polluted, and restore it to its essential beauty and magnificence, it will inevitably collapse on us in heaps of wreckage."[43]

***

In conclusion, then, what alternative solution does Gülen's thought provide us to save others and in turn us? This essay suggests a paradigmatic re-consideration of our-*selves* in terms of nature/other. In particular, Gülen's love-centric worldview helps our *self*-reflection of the separation thesis between self and others that we have long taken for granted, and thereby would lead us to find an alternative paradigm. For instance, an answer to the question if we perceive nature as an alienated other subjected to our privileged-*selves* may be found in Gülen's thought of self and others, which suggests 'a dialogical self' whose existence harmoniously interacts with others and to whom nature exists as a dialogically organic other and an object of love and care.

---

[43] Ibid.

THE GÜLEN MOVEMENT:
CULTIVATING ECO-JUSTICE
THROUGH EDUCATION
AND SELF-REFASHIONING

MARGARET RAUSCH

Eco-justice refers to global economic and ecological justice, understood as an objective for addressing deteriorating social and environmental conditions and ultimately promoting peace in the world among human communities and between human communities and the ecosystem. First coined in 1973, the term emerged out of lessons drawn from the oppressive conditions of imperialism and environmental disasters. To religious and secular advocates of eco-justice, education is essential for promoting social justice and ecological integrity.

The engaged Muslim thinker and educator Fethullah Gülen has written extensively on education, encompassing the overall development of the individual, from early childhood socialization through formal education, comprising training in affect, reason, morality and spirituality, offered through the dispositions, attitudes and values that implicitly inform the pedagogical methodology and comportment of the teacher. Among these dispositions, attitudes and values are altruism, humility and generosity, as well as compassion and sense of responsibility for and the desire to serve all of humanity. Peace is a central goal of Gülen's vision, to be pursued through dialogue activities headed by ethically, emotionally and spiritually advanced guides. The resulting harmonious and compassionate interaction is further cultivated through communal spiritual interconnectedness (*şahs-ı manevi*), which proliferates expectations of justice and accountability worldwide, fostering multi-level problem resolution.

My paper investigates these ideas as articulated in Gülen's writings and implemented by affiliates of the movement inspired by him, the Gülen movement or Hizmet (Service). It explores this implementation by drawing on responses collected during in-depth interviews with seven men and women affiliates, studying or working in Gülen -inspired schools or other unrelated institutions in the US. It examines their perspectives on the process by which they refashion themselves in preparation for service (*hizmet*) and on their embodiment of Gülen's ideas in their daily lives and work, particularly those related to the pursuit of eco-justice.

Eco-Justice: Conceptualization and Implementation

Eco-justice as a concept developed in the early 1970s in conversations about the causes of the ecological decline and oppression that had brought suffering to segments of the human community. First defined by Boston University School of Theology professor Norman Faramelli in 1973 as "the simultaneous concern for social justice and environmental quality plus their interrelationships,"[1] it was eventually understood as a broader framework or "paradigm for doing ethics" in the late 20th and early 21st century, through which the elements of the "fractured and fragmented world" are viewed as "a whole."[2] This vision has encouraged secular and religious social justice advocates and environmentalists to unite and collaborate in pursuit of solutions. Regardless of perspective, the majority has concurred that the solution lies in the realm of education.

Significant early milestones in the development of approaches to the promotion of social justice, which provided part of the impetus for the later eco-justice initiatives, include Brazilian educator and influential theorist of critical pedagogy Paolo Freiere's 1970 publication *Pedagogy of the Oppressed* and the Paulo Freire Institute established in São Paulo in 1991 to extend and elaborate his theory of popular education. The objective of Freire's pedagogy was to instill in those trapped within the confines of limited situations the need to gain consciousness of the root structures by which they were bound. He felt that by raising people's consciousness of the limitations that they faced resulting from the local and global infrastructures informing their lives, particularly those characterized by oppressive tactics, they could eventually act on the possibilities that such infrastructures veiled.[3] His work eventually spawned a movement providing the impetus and theoretical underpinning for later secular and faith-based initiatives to address environmental issues, social

---

[1] Norman Faramelli, "The Role of the Church in Eco-Justice," *Church and Society* 64 (1973): 1-22.
[2] Peter W. Bakken, "Freedom, Equality, and Community in the Eco-Justice Literature," *The Journal of Liberal Religion* 1:2 (2000).
[3] Richard V. Kahn,. "Paulo Freire and Eco-Justice: Updating Pedagogy of the Oppressed for the Age of Ecological Calamity," *Freire Online Journal* 1:1 (2003): 1-20.

justice violations or both, which have in turn given rise to activities, websites and printed materials. One outgrowth was the ecopedagogy movement, whose mission is to develop an appreciation for the collective potentials of being human and to foster social justice worldwide, as part of a future-oriented eco-political vision. The goal of this vision was to realize culturally relevant forms of knowledge grounded in such normative concepts as sustainability, planetarity (identification as earthlings) and biophilia (love of all life). In his forthcoming book *Ecopedagogy: Educating for Sustainability in Schools and Society*, Richard Kahn effectively elucidates the role of ecopedagogy in guiding schools, educational policy, and institutional culture in advancing eco-justice education. Today, films, books, and websites promoting eco-justice education from a non-religious perspective abound.

Governance is the centerpiece of an approach for addressing environmental issues and social inequity situated at the global level. As part of the vision of the human community as one entity, which emerged with the founding of the United Nations, the Earth Charter constitutes one of many projects based on international collaboration, in this case in the pursuit of eco-justice worldwide. The Earth Charter was drafted through a six-year worldwide consultation process (1994-2000) engaging actors from all over the world and overseen by the independent Earth Charter Commission. It was approved at a meeting of the Earth Charter Commission at the UNESCO headquarters in Paris in March 2000 and formally endorsed by organizations and religious communities that represent millions of people worldwide. In his article on the charter, J. Ronald Engel (2007) undertakes a reassessment of its inherent intent and value. Examining its language closely, he demonstrates that the charter is grounded in democratic faith rather than procedural democracy. The latter has flourished, he asserts, in conjunction with "commercial cultures, exclusive social bonds, imperial ambitions, and defiance of natural limits," amply demonstrating the "all too-human efforts to escape the moral burdens of public life by the duplicitous substitution of bargaining for deliberation, our tendencies to paranoia, apathy, and over-indulgence of the appetites, and our readiness to withdrawal into islands of sectarian self-righteousness." [4] He demonstrates that the charter "strongly affirms twentieth century doctrines of universal human rights" and "retrieves strands within the democratic tradition that have been muted in recent years, in particular, our common humanity, the embeddedness of the

---

[4] J. Ronald Engel, "The Earth Charter as a New Covenant for Democracy," *Religion and Culture Web Forum* (2007): 5-6.

human community within the order of nature, and the dependence of politics and ethics upon a substantive ontology or conception of the good." Furthermore, the charter "draws extensively upon understandings of environmental ethics that have grown out of modern democratic moral traditions, such as the land ethic and responsible resource conservation" and "boldly sets forth the new and radical democratic claim that all citizens bear 'a universal responsibility' for the perpetual flourishing of the whole of life on planet Earth."[5] Engel asserts that the charter's vision of a solution is grounded in the development of dispositions and values such as humility and compassion[6] and the promotion of what he refers to as a universal, holistic, and transcendent democratic faith.[7]

Similarly, some Christian churches, groups and thinkers have sought solutions in the scripture and basic theological concepts. One example is National Council of Churches' (2005) God's Earth is Sacred: An Open Letter to Church and Society, posted on the Eco-Justice Ministries' website (http://www.eco-justice.org), which advocates the cultivation of dispositions such as humility, frugality, generosity and compassion. Another example is Noel Preston's response to existing strategies promoting eco-justice, entailing a reframing of four characteristics of Christianity, which he designates as "neo-Christian eco-theology." The first characteristics is exclusivism which must be replaced by inclusivism not only vis-à-vis gender, race or species, but also with regard to the recognition "that the 'truth to live by' may be revealed in varying and multiple ways," thus rejecting "fundamentalist" mindsets. Secondly, he espouses the mystical rather than literalist dimension of Christianity, emphasizing "an experience of transcendence which is connected to life's mysteries and uncertainties" and "triggered by connectedness with the cosmic community of life." Thirdly, he advocates for an eco-centric as opposed to an anthropocentric approach, rejecting "human-centered theology, which subtly endorses our species' destructive dominance of nature through human technology in favor of a view which takes seriously the intrinsic value of all life." Finally, his neo-Christian eco-theology is "shaped by an over-riding sense of the goodness of life rather than its undeniable tragedy," asserting "that life's purpose is more about celebrating

---

[5] Ibid., 4.
[6] Ibid., 13 and 22.
[7] Ibid., 3.

original goodness." [8] In sum, Preston highlights Christian values that promote the embrace of eco-justice.

Christian and other faith-based groups have developed similar approaches, and instructional programs for their implementation, using websites to disseminate information. Examples grounded in Buddhism include Vipassana (http://www.dhamma.org), which centers on meditation as the centerpiece of its "art of living," and Soka Gakkai International (http://www.sgi.org), which promotes meditative chanting practices and dialogue for bridging cultural divides and seeking solutions to global problems facing humanity. This brief examination of eco-justice activism shows that regardless of the perspectives of their originators, many approaches to the promotion of eco-justice and modes for their implementation center on pedagogy, understood as encompassing formal public education, religious instruction and adult instructional opportunities, and on local and global institutional reform. Whether grounded in theology or political philosophy, they are often informed by a recognized need for a deep-seated, thoroughgoing systemic alteration. Thinkers and activists alike acknowledge the necessity for an accompanying mindset or worldview transformation, a process encompassing emotional, psychological, intellectual, and spiritual dimensions.

Gülen's Vision: Cultivating Eco-Justice through Education

Fethullah Gülen has been writing and speaking for several decades about education as a means of guidance towards addressing world problems. The thoughts and feelings expressed in his extensive oral and written production have been implemented in a variety of ways, giving rise to activities, forums, institutions and enterprises that promote education understood in the broadest sense. This variety reflects the complexity and multidimensionality of Gülen's vision. His writings contain guidance for education at all levels from the initial phases of upbringing through formal education and beyond. Important to his vision is a mode of education intended specifically for movement affiliates. It entails a self-refashioning process that comprises three interwoven and interdependent dimensions for cultivating attributes, values and dispositions inspired by the Islamic foundational texts, the Qur'an and Hadith (the Prophet Muhammad's

---

[8] Noel Preston, "Exploring Eco-justice: Reframing Ethics and Spirituality in the Context of Globalization. St Francis' Theological College," *Occasional Papers* 13 (2001): 6.

words and deeds). The three dimensions include: 1) growth and renewal through language, thought and action, 2) the cultivation of dispositions, attitudes and virtues, including humility, compassion and responsibility for all of creation, and 3) communal interconnectedness.

In Gülen's view, education during the first two phases, upbringing in the home and schooling, encompasses responsibilities shared by men and women. Women as mothers are the initial primary nurturers and educators in the child's life, but men are encouraged to follow Muhammad's example by providing affection, care and guidance to their children.[9] Both parents educate their children through their words and deeds, which should reflect their values and principles. In Gülen's understanding, role modeling is central to education at all levels. Schoolteachers are responsible in this regard in the next phase of education, which encompasses much more than simply imparting knowledge.

> The real teacher... is occupied with what is good and wholesome, and to lead and guide the child in his or her life and in the face of all events... [The] child is cast in his or her true mould and attains to the mysteries of personality.... [I]magination and aspirations, or specific skills and realities, everything acquired must... be the key to closed doors, and a guidance to the ways to virtue.... [This] enables pupils to connect happenings in the outer world to their inner experience... [As] intermediaries, teachers... provide the link between life and the self... [They] find a way to the heart of the pupil and leave indelible imprints upon his or her mind. Teachers... will be able to provide good examples for their pupils and teach them the aims of the sciences... through the refinement of their own minds... Patience is of great importance in education. Educating people is the most sacred, but also the most difficult, task in life. In addition to setting a good personal example, teachers should be patient... They should know their students well, and address their intellects and their hearts, spirits, and feelings... [and] show special concern for every individual, not forgetting that each individual is a different "world."[10]

Gülen emphasizes the importance of developing this individuality and its multiple facets in the first two phases of education. His writings on this phase provide guidance for parents and for those affiliates, who will serve in Gülen-inspired schools.[11]

---

[9] Gülen, *The Essentials of the Islamic Faith*, trans. Ali Ünal (Fairfax, VA: The Fountain, 2000).
[10] Gülen, "Our Education System," 2006, www.fethullahgulen.org.
[11] Enes Ergene, "Community and the Concept of Collective Personality," 2008, www.fethullahgulen.org.

Education after the initial phases of schooling takes place naturally in society. Among movement affiliates, it is supplemented by self-refashioning, which constitutes an individual and communally supported endeavor. Self-refashioning aims at developing one's propensity for a wide range of disposition, attitudes and virtues, including self-supervision (*muraqaba*), self-scrutiny (*muhasaba*) and limiting one's relationship to material things (*zuhd*), a lifelong process entailing continuous conscious self-renewal. Advancement equips affiliates with the capacity to contribute to the resolution of today's societal problems, which have given rise to widespread animosity and lack of tolerance and which are linked to excessive materialism.[12] Gülen advocates self-refashioning as a means to revitalize emphatic acceptance (*hoşgörü*) and compassion, which are central to true humanism. His approach entails empowering one's spirituality against the carnal self (*nefis*), instead of shunning the material world. Others constitute one's equals, not opposites, and promoting harmonious co-existence and dialogue is central to self-refashioning and to the discovery of one's "true identity" and capacity for pursuing development toward completion as a human being.

For the first dimension, continuous growth and renewal through thought, language and action, Gülen draws inspiration from the Qur'an, specifically from autodidactic and self-referential verses such as the following in envisioning self-refashioning.

> God has sent down the best discourse as a Book, fully consistent within itself, often repeated, it causes the skins of those who fear their Lord to shiver; then their skins and hearts soften to the remembrance of God. (39: 23)

> Judgment Day is approaching. None but God can make it manifest. With this Qur'an are you not amazed? And laughing? And weeping? How can you still be arrogant? So prostrate yourselves before God and worship Him. (53: 57-62)

In two writings,[13] Gülen expounds upon the function of emotional arousal elicited through listening to or reciting the Qur'an in enhancing conviction and commitment to obligatory ritual practices and ethical comportment and in cultivating emotional and spiritual dispositions, attitudes and virtues. Moreover, his vast corpus with its poetic elaboration of Islamic

---

[12] Gülen, *The Essentials of Islamic Faith.*
[13] Gülen, *Kur'an'ın Altın İkliminde* (*In the Golden Climate of the Qur'an*), 1997, www.fethullahgulen.org and *Speech and Power of Expression: On Language, Esthetics, and Belief* (Clifton: Tughra Books, 2010).

doctrine and practice in Turkish language serves to replicate this didactic function for speakers of Turkish. His acknowledgement of the importance of language and of its role in the development of knowledge, ideas, thoughts, speech and culture is articulated in the following excerpt from a short writing entitled Language and Thought.

> Language is one of the fundamental dynamics in the composition of a culture. Language is an important tool for humankind in our efforts to better understand the cosmos and events both holistically and analytically. The more richly and colorfully a nation can speak, the more they can think; the more they can think, the broader is the span their speech can reach. Every single society leaves behind what they speak and think today for its validity to be probed, tested, and protected by future generations. In this way, a huge reserve of experience and learning are saved from being wasted; the knowledge and ideas of the past are utilized for the benefit of the present; what was right or wrong in the past is compared with the rights and wrongs of today so that we do not tread the same path and suffer from the same errors. This is valid for all nations of the world; the capacity of a language to express a thought is related to the level of development it has achieved, and a thought can become the instrument by which the language is tuned to this level of development. From every aspect, language plays a defining role in the formation of our culture.[14]

Though discussed in relation to societies and nations, these ideas apply equally to the community of movement affiliates. This excerpt reveals Gülen's intent to transmit values from the past to benefit the future and to contribute to the formation of a new culture. The new culture is transmitted by way of a new language, the poetic and metaphorical language characterizing his works on which the spiritual and emotional development of the affiliates depends. His works includes book-length works but also shorter writings. The books commonly read by affiliates include *Sonsuz Işık*, or *The Infinite Light* (2002), a study of the Prophet's life and roles in the early community, and *Kalbin Zümrüt Tepeleri*, or *The Emerald Hills of the Heart* (2003), a study of the dispositions, attitudes and virtues cultivated in self-refashioning. These and other works by Gülen, available in print and on the movement website in Turkish and in English translation, provide affiliates with background and grounding in the Qur'an and Islamic doctrine, as well as elaborations on their application in daily life. They are also encouraged to read *Sözler*, or *Words* (2002), a work by Gülen's teacher, the renowned Kurdish Islamic scholar, Said Nursi, which centers on lessons elucidating and applying aspects of

---

[14] Gülen, "Language and Thought," 2008, www.fethullahgulen.org.

Islamic doctrine in daily life. Affiliates read and discuss the works in *sohbetler*, or gatherings headed by an advanced affiliate, referred to as *abla* (big sister) or *abi* (big brother). *Sohbetler* also serve as forums for discussing spiritual experiences related to self-refashioning and for viewing video recordings of Gülen's sermons. Viewing video recordings of Gülen's sermons, or listening to cassette recordings of them, also enables affiliates to stay connected with Gülen, emotionally, spiritually and intellectually. The short writings include articles found in periodicals, such as *Sızıntı: Aylık Ilim-Kültür Dergisi*, or *Trickling: A Monthly Science-Culture Magazine*, which contains two articles written by Gülen and the rest by advanced affiliates. The first, at the beginning of the magazine, focuses on a variety of topics, such as religious holidays, and the second, in the middle, is drawn from *Emerald Hills of the Heart*. The language of the articles is metaphorical and poetic. Remaining connected with Gülen's thoughts, language and style perpetuates self-refashioning.

The role of thought and action, and their interrelationship, in self-refashioning is the subject of other writings by Gülen.

> [T]he way to true existence is action and thought, and likewise the way to renewal, individual and collective…Action in this context then means embracing the whole of creation with full sincerity and resolve, aware of journeying to an eternal realm…; it means expending all one's physical, intellectual and spiritual faculties in guiding the world to undertake the same journey…As for thought, it is action in one's inner world. Any truly systematic thinking entails seeking answers to all questions arising from the existence of the universe as such. In other words, truly systematic thinking is the product of a conscious mind relating itself to the whole of creation and seeking the truth in everything through its language.[15]

Here again the language, which he is proliferating, the language of truth, is instrumental, in seeking and recognizing the truth. Thought and action are integral to self-refashioning, and self-refashioning prepares affiliates for *hizmet*, or service. In addition, the performance of *hizmet* advances self-refashioning, which is an ongoing lifelong process. Movement affiliates, referred to by Gülen as the golden or awaited generation "unite in [their] character profound spirituality, wide knowledge, sound thinking, a scientific temperament, and wise activism." "Never content with what [they] already know, [they] will continuously increase in knowledge, knowledge of the self, knowledge of nature, and knowledge of God."[16] They attain "true life" by applying the attributes developed through self-

---

[15] Gülen, "Action and Thought," 2006, www.fethullahgulen.org.
[16] Gülen, "The Awaited Generation," 2006, www.fethullahgulen.org.

refashioning, as the following quote explains: "The true life is the one lived at the spiritual level. There is a mutually supportive and perfective relation between one's actions and inner life... a 'virtuous circle.'"[17] "True life" is attained through intense individual work on oneself, which comprises the second dimension.

The second dimension of self-refashioning, cultivating dispositions, attitudes and virtues, is an individual endeavor comprising reading Gülen's writings and implementing their guidance. In the following passage, Gülen describes some of the dispositions, attitudes and virtues and the benefits of cultivating them as well as tendencies that prevail in their absence.

> Helplessness, poverty, affection, reflection, zeal and thankfulness are the basic elements of the way {of the Prophet's Companions to reach the ranks and stations and the favors and blessings that come through spiritual journeying and suffering}. Helplessness means being aware of one's inability to do many of the things that one wants to do, and poverty denotes the awareness of the fact that it is God Who is the real Owner and Master of everything. Embracing everybody and everything because of Him is affection, while reflection is thinking deeply, analytically and systematically about and meditating on the outer and inner world, with a new excitement everyday. Zeal is the great, ardent desire and yearning to reach God and to serve in His way. Always thanking God for His bounties and proceeding to Him in full consciousness of all His blessings during the journey is thankfulness...
>
> A person with an unpurified, evil-commanding carnal self may be forgetful of the most vital matters, which should never be forgotten, and such a person does not even want to recollect them, while pulling up from the heart matters that should never be remembered. Human beings should always think of serving God's cause, of being earnest in their deeds, of their responsibilities to the people around them, and of death and what lies beyond it. They should uproot from their spirits hatred, jealousy, worldly ambitions, greed, and carnal desires. Only by doing so can human beings keep their innate tendency toward spirituality alive, and refrain from rousing the satanic tendencies within themselves.[18]

In the following passage, he elucidates other dispositions, attitudes and virtues that characterize members of what he refers to as the "awaited, golden generation," in other words movement affiliates who have attained advanced stages in the self-refashioning process.

---

[17] Gülen, "Balancing the Spiritual and the Physical," 2008, www.fethullahgulen.org.
[18] Gülen, "Another Way of Journeying and Initiation," 2007, www.fethullahgulen.org.

Attitudes like determination, perseverance, and resolve illuminate their inner conscience, and the brightness of this inner conscience strengthens their willpower and resolve, stimulating him or her to ever-higher horizons. [They] will always seek to please the Creator and serve humanity... {They will} fulfill their duties meticulously and thoroughly, attend with care to every little detail, and enjoy orderliness, harmony, and devotion to duty in their outer worlds. At the same time, they increase the pure light of their inner worlds... Their intellects can combine... all current knowledge... and thereby obtain new syntheses. They are so modest that they see themselves as just ordinary people among others. Finally, their altruism has reached such a level that they can forget their own needs and desires for the sake of others' happiness.[19]

The following passage elucidates the potential for transforming the world realizable by advanced affiliates.

Just as a rosebud turned towards light unfurls into an elaborate flower, so we, in the past, appeared as a great nation in the historical and international arena after we turned towards and embraced our religion. This overall self-attainment caused our potentials to develop and secured our existence for centuries. Again, just as our existence and self-attainment depend on attachment to our religion and its values, our integration with the whole of creation requires the same, as was the case in the past. Indeed, every act of a believer is worship, his every thought self-discipline, his every speech a supplication expressing his degree of knowledge of God, his every observation a research, and his relations with others a grounding in love and compassion...

Those who are planning the happy world of the future should be aware of what kind of world they mean to build, what sort of jewels they should use in its construction, so that they will not have, later, to destroy with their own hands what their own hands built. Equipped with rational thought and religious values and historical dynamics, they should know how to apply the principles of the Qur'an and Sunnah {Prophetic Example or Hadith} and the judgments derived from them by conscientious scholars, to the world they intend to build. They should never be given over to carnal appetites and temporary aspirations...

[T]he realization of such noble aims depends on the existence of guides and leaders able to both diagnose our external and inner misery and to be themselves in constant relation with the higher worlds.... Thus, all the institutions of life will be remoulded.... Sciences will progress hand-in-hand with religion, and belief and reason combined will yield ever-fresh fruits of their cooperation. In short, the future will witness a new world built in the arms of hope, belief, love, knowledge, and resolve.[20]

[19] Gülen, "Balancing the Spiritual and the Physical."
[20] Gülen, "Action and Thought."

In Gülen's view, self-refashioning will enable the awaited, golden generation to resolve societal and world problems.

The third dimension, communal interconnectedness, encompasses several components including role modeling, companionship, community and *şahs-ı manevi*. Role modeling, or learning by observing and following the example of peers and advanced affiliates, is important to self-refashioning. It occurs through companionship and communal interaction, both of which are essential to organizing and carrying out *hizmet* activities. *Şahs-ı manevi*, a central aspect of all of these components, refers to communal spiritual interconnectedness. A member of Gülen's inner circle describes *şahs-ı manevi* as follows.

> Sufism is present in the Gülen movement... in the form of... their emphasis...on the collective personality, or *şahs-ı manevi*. This emphasis acknowledges the community to be a corporate body that shares spiritual unity and personality. This body is a collective representation of a unified system of willpower, idea, beliefs, and behaviors. Communal principles emerge as concrete forms of these unifying wills and efforts. Like a piece of ice melting in the ocean and thus becoming the ocean, every person degrades his ego to become one with the collective spiritual personality. Partaking in this spiritual unity means that one should leave behind, or at least not give priority to, his or her personal interests, pleasures, and engagements. This happens primarily in areas where the community expects action from its participants. The formation of a collective personality shapes around the principle of spreading the word of God. All communal activities, rituals, values, principles, and goals intend for this aim. The ideal of spreading the word of God to all of humankind requires the efforts of both single individuals and the collective body of the community.[21]

Şahs-ı manevi, Ergene asserts, refers to the conscious and unconscious unification of community members' wills and efforts through the renunciation of the individual for the sake of the community. Heon Kim offers an excellent detailed elaboration of its spiritual dimensions, elucidating its connections to Sufism and the historical Turkish tradition, as articulated in Gülen's writings. Being interconnected with co-affiliates by collectively carrying out activities, observing each other's behavior and exchanging thoughts and ideas about their behavior and activities is understood to have didactic import.

---

[21] Ergene, Community and the Concept of Collective Personality.

In Gülen's view, education is integrally linked to *hizmet*, which refers to service to humanity solely in the pursuit of God's satisfaction. Education in all its facets prepares the individual for *hizmet*, which in turn fosters further progress toward the spiritual, emotional, psychological, intellectual and ethical perfection that is encompassed by his understanding of education. Central to education is interaction and dialogue, which are linked to role modeling, or offering an example through one's words and deeds and learning from the example of others, with the Prophet serving as the ultimate exemplary model. This sharing and exchange occurs at a practical level, but also in the realm of the unconscious, as part of *şahs-ı manevi*, or the communal spiritual interconnectedness, ensuring the further proliferation of the acquired and practiced emotional, psychological, intellectual, spiritual and ethical dispositions, attitudes and virtues. All three dimensions of self-refashioning foster the development of moral selfhood and compassionate engagement, which are essential to endeavoring to attain a state of completeness as a human being and to living as a responsible member of society, locally and globally, a sense of responsibility oriented toward God.[22] In Gülen's vision, all aim at realizing God's plan of establishing of peace and harmony for all of creation.

Implementing Gülen's Vision: Self-Refashioning and Eco-Justice

The implementation of Gülen's vision entails a multi-dimensional, individualized, and emotional self-refashioning process illuminated here in the responses offered by seven affiliates of the Gülen movement. These responses, collected during in-depth interviews conducted in September and October of 2010 offer personal experiences of self-refashioning, a process that is central to acquiring and applying emotional, psychological, intellectual, spiritual and ethical dispositions, attitudes and virtues prescribed by Gülen as essential for pursuing the above-mentioned goals. The interviewees are designated by letters of the alphabet (A through G) to protect their identities, and their backgrounds are characterized in general terms. Of the seven who all currently reside in the US, one is from Azerbaijan, one is from Kazakhstan, and the rest are from Turkey, four are women, and five are married with between one and three children. They include a temporarily professionally inactive first-time mother, wife and teacher in a Gülen-inspired school, a holder of an American BA with

[22] Simon Robinson, "Fethullah Gülen and the Concept of Responsibility," 2008, www.fethullahgulen. org.

honors, who is currently applying to professional schools, a PhD student on scholarship, a PhD student with a university research position, a teacher in Gülen-inspired school and a high-level professional seeking a new employment opportunity after relocation within the US. Their affiliation experience varies widely from one who was raised by movement affiliate parents to one whose has been affiliated for only five years. The affiliates responses are organized according to the three dimensions of self-refashioning elaborate above with the addition of a fourth dimension, its relationship to the promotion of eco-justice. These four dimensions informed the open-ended interview questions.

The first topic probed by the questions was the role of language, thought and action in self-refashioning. The seven interviewees agreed that all three were important, and that they were interrelated. Two interviewees responded as follows.

> It {self-refashioning} is the result of so many factors over so many years that it is difficult for me to explain. In general, it Hocaefendi's {affectionate appellation for Gülen meaning respected teacher} words and actions, the way he preaches and lives, his thoughts and ideas, that have had a huge impact on me, emotionally, spiritually and mentally. I try to reproduce them through my words and actions, and to live by what I think and say like he does. He is brilliant, sincere and deeply emotional. He opens people's horizons with his words and ideas. (A)

> Being a part of Hizmet {the Gülen Movement} changed my outlook on life. I see so many things differently and understand them better. All the beauty in my life emerged from my involvement, from reading, discussing ideas with other Hizmet people, trying to be a better Muslim, and serving other people. It definitely shaped my personality. My ways of thinking and attitudes changed and my life now has meaning and direction. Materialism, money, home, and car are not my first priority anymore. I discovered that spirituality and service are very satisfying. The feelings I experienced when being more tolerant towards people, loving them and offering them help transformed me. An important aim of Hizmet is sharing ideas with other people. This requires speaking, learning to formulate your thoughts and express your feelings. In general, one could say that Hizmet is a way of life. (B)

One of affiliates emphasized the aspect of constant renewal, the gradual but continuous nature of the self-refashioning process. She illustrated it using water as a metaphor.

> Self-refashioning is a life long process with many facets. Each person organizes it as needed, since it is focused on the individual person. It

consists of reading, thinking, discussing, scrutinizing yourself and serving other people and God. The way I learned to approach it is to think about it as a step-by-step and day-by-day endeavor. You can observe your progress and correct things all the time as you go along. The important thing to remember is that you need to strive to do better the next time and that progress is the main point. You can usually do things better the second time. There might be bad days, but they are also good for learning about what went wrong and why. It is like a bucket with a hole. If a bucket filled with water stands for a long time the water will get stale, dirty and unclear. But a bucket with a hole will lose its water gradually and the water needs to be replenished. By regularly replenishing the water, you are also making sure that it is fresh, clean and clear. Your ability to behave following Hocaefendi's guidance requires you to refresh your knowledge by reading, thinking and observing and by sharpening your skills at performing *hizmet* through practice and self-scrutiny. (F)

In these narratives, the affiliates recount their experiences with the back and forth movement between thought and action, guided by the new language and ideas acquired from reading Gülen's works. They underscored the gradual and continuous nature of self-refashioning.

The interviewees mentioned a number of dispositions, attitudes and virtues and explained their importance to self-refashioning and the means for their acquisition as follows.

Hizmet people abide in a kind of process, first of all within themselves. Mentally, spiritually and emotionally, they question themselves. Only after diligently performing self-criticism, can they begin a new period of remaking their inner selves and applying what they learn to their lives. They read about, discuss and try to perform all the new values and behaviors, such as humility, emphatic acceptance, compassion and self-sacrifice as often as they can. Self-criticism helps them to watch and evaluate their progress. (D)

In Hizmet, you are constantly striving to be a better person. You try to develop new attitudes and behaviors. These include altruism, tolerance, humility, self-sacrifice, compassion, and responsibility for yourself and your family, but also for others around you. To do this, you read about these attitudes and behaviors in Hocaefendi's books and then you think about how to practice them in your life. You try them out, observe yourself doing them and think about how well or badly you did. The next time you have a chance you try again. You can also talk to other Hizmet people about your progress. It's a long slow process full of struggle and satisfaction. The satisfaction comes from knowing that you are helping others and making their lives easier and happier, and, most importantly, that you are serving God. (C)

These narratives elucidate the complexity and importance of the individual dimension of self-refashioning and its relationship with the two other dimensions.

The interviewees offered the following recollections and thoughts in response to questions about companionship, community, role modeling and communal spiritual interconnectedness.

> I met Gülen people eight years ago when I was a first-year college student. I was living in a dormitory that belongs to Hizmet. At first, I could not get used to these people readily since I was prejudice against them because the media was harshly criticizing Gülen. When people were listening to him preaching, I tried to ignore him. Then I asked myself a question: What do I want to become in the future and the answer was: A good professor. I told myself that I would have to learn about my own culture and religion in order to become a good professor/person. When I got rid of my earlier prejudice against Gülen and listened to his sermons and read his books, I was amazed and inspired by his meaningful words. The *abiler* became my role models. They read religious books, performed good deeds, and were very altruistic, humble, pious and honest. At the time, I continued to play basketball with old friends, guys with long hair and earrings. One day, I asked myself "Do you want to become like Gülen people or these guys?" The answer was definitely like Gülen people. After that, my love towards Gülen people started. In the *ışık evler*, the *abiler* are real guides. They ignore your wrongdoings and try to help you. Sometimes, they stay up at night pondering other people's problems. I didn't know much about Islam and had long hair when I first met these people, but they did not criticize me. They loved me for who I am, and I eventually loved them for who they are. Now I love, share and grow with other affiliates. We serve as examples in everything we do and support each other. (B)

> Some emotional and spiritual experiences, in affiliate gatherings in home and especially in camp settings, had an important impact on me. I was affected emotionally in these settings where large groups of affiliates were regularly performing prayers, trying to learn from reading books and striving to be a perfect person. When you are surrounded by living examples of altruism and compassion becoming filled with the desire to devote yourself to serving others is unavoidable. The trust you feel in others, people inside and outside the movement, increases with time as you perfect your performance of *hizmet*. So does the trust they place in you. Your relationships with them get better over time. The relationships, mutual observation, interaction and shared participation in activities, are very important. Equally important is the feeling of being a part of the whole. Each person is of little significance by him or herself, but essential to the group. Group belonging, interaction and atmosphere are essential to self-refashioning. (G)

Hizmet would not be Hizmet without living examples. Others serve as your models until you are ready to serve as a model too, but learning from each other is never finished. It's a gradual, continuous and multi-faceted process, which connects the individual and the community on many levels, emotional, intellectual and spiritual. You grow and mature by interacting in an environment of sharing, exchange, dialogue and compassion. It is also central to interaction with non-affiliates as a way of teaching them about our ideas and values. (F)

As indicated in the narratives, the process is individual, but also integrally dependent on group belonging, interaction and support.

The final topic of the interviews was the movement's potential for promoting eco-justice. The interviewees offered the following reflections and insights from readings and sermons.

Gülen sincerely loves all of God's creation. He cries when he thinks about the smallest suffering of an ant and when he sees a leaf fall from a tree. If we learn to be more like Gülen, and teach others to be like him too, we will be promoting love for nature, and all of creation. This is the way Hizmet people can promote eco-justice. (A)

The Prophet Muhammad forbade his followers from destroying the property of the people they fought in battle, including their houses, fields and trees. He encouraged people to plant trees and care for them. Hizmet people try to imitate Muhammad. They can encourage eco-justice by following the Prophet's example. (B)

Moderation is important in Islam. Wasting is unacceptable. Eco-justice is against wasting energy. As good Muslims, Hizmet people can contribute to eco-justice by teaching people not to waste anything, including energy. (C)

Hizmet people try to show compassion for all people and teach others to be compassionate. They hope that their example will spread to all human beings. If everyone learns compassion, they will be good to each other. Gülen says that there are enough resources, including food and energy for all people. If all humans learn to love each other like Gülen is trying to teach them to do, then there will be no more hunger or related problems. People will share everything and help each other in every way. When these problems end, war and misunderstanding will end too, and the world will be a better place. People will live in peace and harmony. (D)

I think Hizmet people are promoting eco-justice in small ways. Gülen has written about planting trees. He suggested that people plant trees to celebrate important events like the birth of a child, graduation from high school and marriage. If everyone could learn about Gülen's ideas and follow his advice, they would spend time planting trees and caring for them, and taking care of other things in nature. The deserts would become smaller and the climate would improve. People would be good to each other. They would be happier and live in harmony. (E)

Hizmet people are contributing to eco-justice indirectly. They are following Gülen and trying to live by his ideas. I believe that he is working towards eco-justice in his own way. Gülen teaches us to be better human beings and to help other people to be good and happy too. Goodness and happiness are contagious. When we interact with other people, we try to help them and teach them the value of spreading goodness and happiness. Hizmet people love and care for all of God's creation. It's a kind of spiritual approach to eco-justice. (F)

Hizmet is apolitical. Politics is about having an opinion and rejecting other opinions. Hizmet is about accepting and loving everyone. For this reason, it is not an organization in the true sense. There are no rules, just principles. Anyone who accepts the principles can join. People join and leave voluntarily. They leave if they can't accept the principles. Hizmet people strive to perfect themselves. They try to learn and practice such values as altruism, tolerance, humility, justice, service to humanity, and compassion and responsibility for all human beings. These values and our service make us happy. People we meet can feel all of this and begin to learn from us. They feel connected to us indirectly. To learn these values you have to get control of your carnal desires, your carnal self. When it is out of control, it is attracted to greed, selfishness, animosity, intolerance, hatred and violence. These emotions are what cause the problems in the world, such as social, economic and ecological injustice. I think we can say that Gülen and Hizmet people are for eco-justice. They may even be 'promoting' eco-justice, because they are spreading an atmosphere, feelings and actions that are all about peace, dialogue, love, justice and harmony among people and for all of creation. (G)

As these narratives reveal, the affiliates consider their involvement in the Gülen movement to be a means for contributing directly and indirectly to eco-justice.

The seven affiliates acknowledged the complexity of the self-refashioning process, and the interrelationship between its three dimensions. All three dimensions in interaction foster self-refashioning, as the affiliates elucidated. All seven hold the conviction that the main Islamic and Sufi values and principles, promoted by Gülen as part of self-refashioning, as well as other ideas, preferences and attitudes, related to Islam and originating with the Prophet Muhammad, such as tree-planting as a commemorative act, link the movement's activities to the objectives of eco-justice. *Şahs-ı manevi*, or communal spiritual interconnectedness, is noteworthy as a link, since it constitutes a conscious and unconscious means for sharing and proliferating the values and principles among affiliates, but also between them and the people they serve.

Concluding Remarks

A preliminary examination of scholarship and websites reveal that many advocates of eco-justice seek solutions in education, viewing it as an important means to change mindsets and to acquire dispositions, attitudes and values conducive to eco-justice. Fethullah Gülen's ideas have inspired the formation of a movement whose affiliates have created institutions, activities and practices, which promote channels of education situated in informal frameworks and formal institutions, to directly and indirectly reshape mindsets and foster eventual systemic alteration, gradually from the bottom up. Individuals, who have undergone self-refashioning, or the cultivation of dispositions, attitudes and values, including altruism, humility and compassion for humanity and all of creation, which are considered essential to the new mindset and systemic framework, work within the parameters of these institutions, activities and practices to promote dialogue, harmonious co-existence and peace. *Şahs-ı manevi*, or communal spiritual interconnectedness, one dimension of self-refashioning, enhances the other aspects of that process, but is also understood to be instrumental in awakening in those outside the movement community the desire to collaborate with or be involved in the movement, a global initiative whose goals can be broadly interpreted as contributing to the proliferation of peace and eco-justice worldwide.

BIBLIOGRAPHY

al-Banna, Jamal and Muhammad `Abd al-Salam Faraj. *al-Farīdah al-ghaibah* (Cairo: Dar Thabit, 1984).

Alexander, Paul. *The Byzantine Apocalyptic Tradition* (Berkeley: University of California Press, 1985).

Allport, Gordon. *The Nature of Prejudice* (Cambridge, MA: Addison-Wesley, 1954).

As-Sadr, Muhammad Baqir. *An Inquiry Concerning Al-Mahdi* (Qum, Iran: Ansaryian Publications, n.d).

Attridge, Harold, ed. *HarperCollins Study Bible with Apocrypha and Deuterocanonical Books* (New Revised Standard Version. San Francisco: HarperCollins, 1989).

Bakken, Peter. "Freedom, Equality, and Community in the Eco-Justice Literature." *The Journal of Liberal Religion* 1:2 (2000).

Baskan, Filiz. "The Political Economy of Islamic Finance in Turkey: the role of Fethullah Gülen in Asya Finans." In *The Politics of Islamic Finance,"* Clement M. Henry and Rodney Wilson, eds. (Edinburgh: Edinburgh UniversityPress, 2004).

Benware, Paul. *Understanding the End Times: A Comprehensive Approach* (Chicago: Moody Press, 1995).

Booney, Richard. *Jihād: From Qur'ān to bin Laden* (New York: Palgrave Macmillan, 2004).

Braaten, Carl and Robert Jenson, eds. *Church Dogmatics*. Vol. 2 (Philadelphia: Fortress Press, 1984).

Bukhari, Muhammad ibn Ismaiel. *The Translation of the Meanings of Sahih Al-Bukhari*. Nine Volumes. Muhammad Muhsin Khan, trans (Riyadh: Darussalam, 1997).

Byman, Daniel. "Explaining Ethnic Peace in Morocco," *Harvard Middle Eastern and Islamic Review* 4 (1997):1-29.

Carr, Adrian. "The 'separation thesis' of self and other: metatheorizing a dialectic alternative," *Theory & Psychology* 13:1 (2003): 117-138.

Carroll, Jill. *A Dialogue of Civilizations: Gülen's Islamic Ideals and Humanistic Discourse* (New Jersey: The Light, Inc., 2007).

Çetin, Muhammed. *The Gülen Movement: Civic Service without Borders* (NY: Blue Dome, 2009).

Chidester, David and Edward T. Linenthal, eds., *American Sacred Space* (Bloomington and Indianapolis: Indiana University Press, 1995).

Clausewitz, Carl von. *On War* (London: K. Paul Trench, Trubner, and Co. Ltd., 1911).

Cole, Phillip. *The Myth of Evil: Demonizing the Enemy* (Westport, Conn: Praeger, 2006).

Cook, Stuart. "Experimenting on Social Issues: The Case of School Desegration," American Psychologist 40: 452–460 (1985).

Dawud, Abu. *Sunan Abu Dawud*, Ahmad Hasan, trans. Vol. 3 (Lahore: Sh. Muhammad Ashraf, 2004 reprint).

Dovidio, John and Samuel Gaertner. "Aversive Racism," in Advances in Experimental Social Psychology 36, ed. M. P. Zanna, 1–51 (San Diego: Academic Press, 2004).

Engel, J. Ronald. "The Earth Charter as a New Covenant for Democracy." *Religion and Culture Web Forum* (2007): 1-26.

Esposito, John, ed. *The Oxford Encyclopedia of the Modern Islamic World*, Vol 2 (New York: Oxford University Press, 1995).

Esposito, John and İbrahim Kalın, eds., *The 500 Most Influential Muslims 2009* (Washington, D.C.:Georgetown University Press, 2009).

el Fadl, Khaled Abou. *The Great Theft: Wrestling Islam from the Extremists* (San Francisco: Harper Collins, 2005).

Faramelli, Norman. "The Role of the Church in Eco-Justice." *Church and Society* 64 (1973): 1-22.

Faust, Drew Gilpin. *This Republic of Suffering: Death and the American Civil War* (NY: Knopf, 2008).

Faux, Jeffery. *The Global Class War* (Hoboken, NJ: John Wiley & Sons, Inc., 2006).

Fiorena, Francis Schüssler and John Galvin, eds. *Systematic Theology. Roman Catholic Perspectives*, Vol. 2 (Minneapolis: Fortress Press, 1991).

Foucault, Michel. *The Government of Self and Others: Lectures at the Collège de France 1982-1983,* Arnold I. Davidson, ed., Graham Burchell, trans. (New York: Palgrave Macmillan, 2010).

Freire, Paulo. *Pedagogy of the Oppressed* (New York: Continuum, 1970).

Gülen, M. Fethullah. *Speech and Power of Expression: On Language, Esthetics, and Belief* (Clifton: Tughra Books, 2010).

—. *Toward a Global Civilization of Love And Tolerance.* Foreword by Thomas Michel (Somerset: Tughra Books, 2009).

—."Longing for Love." *The Fountain* 64 (2008).

—."We Should Think Well of Others." *The Fountain* 64 (2008).

—."Compassion." *The Fountain* 63 (2008).

—. *The Essentials of the Islamic Faith* (Somerset: The Light, 2006).

—. *Pearls of Wisdom,* tr. Ali Ünal (NJ: The Light, 2006).

—. *The Essentials of Islamic Faith* (New Jersey: The Light Inc, 2006).

—. "In True Islam, Terror Does Not Exist," in Ergün Capan, ed., *Terror and Suicide Attacks: An Islamic Perspective* (New Jersey: Light, 2005).

—. *The Statue of Our Souls: Revival in Islamic Thought and Activism* (New Jersey: The Light Inc., 2005).

—. *Toward a Global Civilization of Love and Tolerance* (New Jersey: The Light, 2004).

—. *Emerald Hills of the Heart: Key Concepts in the Practice of Sufism 2* (New Jersey: Light, 2004).

—. *Essays, Perspectives, Opinions* (Rutherford, NJ: Fountain, 2002).

—. "The Nature We Have Destroyed," *The Fountain* 15(July – September, 1996).

—. *Baharı Soluklarken* (Izmir: Nil Yayinlari, 1993).

Hanh, Thich Nhat. *Peace is Every Step: The Path of Mindfulness in Everyday Life* (NY: Bantam, 1991).

Hippolytus, "Treatise on Christ and Antichrist" in *Ante-Nicene Fathers,* vol. 5, Alexander Roberts and James Donaldson, eds. (Grand Rapids: Eerdmans, 1957), 204-221.

Holland, Joe and Peter Henriot, *Social Analysis: Linking Faith and Justice* (Maryknoll, NY: Orbis Books, 1983).

Huntington, Samuel. "The Clash of Civilizations," *Foreign Affairs* (Summer 1993): 22-49.

Kahn, Richard V. *Ecopedagogy: Educating for Sustainability in Schools and Society* (New York: Routledge, 2010).

—. "Paulo Freire and Eco-Justice: Updating Pedagogy of the Oppressed for the Age of Ecological Calamity." *Freire Online Journal* 1: 1 (2003): 1-20.

Kazal, Russell A. *Becoming Old Stock: The Paradox of German-American Identity* (Princeton, NJ: Princeton University Press, 2004).

Kelman, Herbert. "Creating the Conditions for Israeli-Palestinian Negotiations," *Journal of Conflict Resolution* 1 (1982): 39-76.

—. "Nationalism, Patriotism, and National Identity: Social-psychological Dimensions." In *Patriotism in the Lives of Individuals and Nations,* D. Bar-Tal and E. Staub, eds. (Chicago: Nelson-Hall, 1997). 165-189.

—. "Negotiating National Identity and Self-Determination in Ethnic Conflicts: The choice between pluralism and ethnic cleansing." *Negotiation Journal* 13 (1997): 327-340.

—. "The Role of National Identity in Conflict Resolution." In *Social Identity, Intergroup Conflict, and Conflict Reduction*, R. D. Ashmore, L. Jussim, & D. Wilder, eds. (Oxford and New York: Oxford University Press, 2001). 187-212.

—. "Interactive Problem Solving: Informal Mediation by the Scholar-Practitioner." In *Studies in international mediation: Essays in honor of Jeffrey Z. Rubin*, J. Bercovitch, ed. (New York: Palgrave Macmillan, 2002), 167-193.

—. "Reconciliation as Identity Change: A Social-Psychological Perspective." In *From Conflict Resolution to Reconciliation*, Y. Bar-Siman-Tov, ed. (Oxford, England: Oxford University Press, 2004), 111-124.

Kim, Heon Choul. "The Nature and Role of Sufism in Contemporary Islam: A Case Study of the Life, Thought and Teachings of Fethullah Gülen" (PhD diss., Temple University, 2008).

Kramer, Martin. "Coming to Terms: Fundamentalists or Islamists?" *Middle East Quarterly* (Spring 2003): 65-77.

Küng, Hans. *Christianity: Essence, History and Future* (New York: Crossroads, 1995).

—. *Islam: Past, Present and Future* (Oxford: Oneworld, 2007).

—. *On Being Christian* (New York: Doubleday, 1976).

LaFreniere, Gilbert. *The Decline of Nature*: *Environmental History and the Western Worldview* (Bethesda, MD : Academica Press, 2008).

Lawrence, Bruce. *Messages to the World: The Statements of Osama Bin Laden* (London: Verso, 2005).

Levinas, Emmanuel. *God, Death, and Time* (Stanford, CA: Stanford University Press, 2000).

Lewis, Bernard. "The Roots of Muslim Rage," *Atlantic Monthly* (September 1990), 60.

Macquarrie, John. *Principles of Christian Theology* (New York: Scribners Sons, 1977).

McFagure, Sallie. *Models of God: Theology for an Ecological, Nuclear Age* (Philadelphia: Fortress Press, 1987).

McGinn, Bernard, John Collins, and Stephen Stein, eds. *Encyclopedia of Apocalypticism*. 3 vols. (New York: Continuum, 1999).

McGinn, Bernard. *Antichrist. Two Thousand Years of the Human Fascination with Evil* (San Francisco: HarperSan Francisco, 1994).

McGrath, Alister. *Christian Theology: An Introduction*. 2nd ed. (Oxford: Blackwells, 1997).

Merchant, Carolyn. *The Death of Nature: Women, Ecology, and the Scientific Revolution* (San Francisco: Harper & Row, 1980).

Mezran, Karim. "Negotiating National Identity in North Africa." *International Negotiation* 2 (2001): 141-173.

Mich, Marvin L. Krier. *Catholic Social Teaching and Movements* (Mystic, CT: Twenty-Third Publications, 1998).

Milanovic, Branko. *Worlds Apart: Measuring International Inequality* (Princeton, NJ: Princeton University Press, 2007).

Miller, N., and M. Brewer, eds. *Groups in Contact: The Psychology of Desegregation* (Orlando, FL: Academic Press, 1984).

Muslim, Abu'l-Husain. *Sahih Muslim*. 4 vols. Abdul Hamid Siddiqi, trans. (New Delhi: Kitab Bhavan, 1986).

Nasr, Seyyed Hossein. "Islam and the Environmental Crisis." In *Spirit and Nature,* Steven C. Rockefeller and John C. Elder, eds. (Boston: Beacon Press, 1992).

Nursi, Said. *The Rays*. Risale-i Nur Collection (Istanbul: Sozler Publications, 2006).

—. *The Letters*. Risale-i Nur Collection (Somerset, NJ, 2007).

—. *The Damascus Sermon* (Istanbul: Nur Publishers, 1989).

Pahl, Jon. *Shopping Malls and Other Sacred Spaces: Putting God in Place* (Grand Rapids: MI: Brazos Press, 2003).

—. *Empire of Sacrifice: The Religious Origins of American Violence* (NY: New York University Press, 2010).

Panayi, Panikos. *The Enemy in our Midst: Germans in Britain during the First World War* (New York: Berg, 1991).

Pettigrew, Thomas. "Intergroup Contact: Theory, Research and New Perspectives," *Annual Review of Psychology* 49: 65–85 (1998).

Pettigrew, Thomas and Tropp, Linda. "Does Intergroup Contact Reduce Prejudice? Recent Meta-analytic Findings." In *Reducing Prejudice and Discrimination*, S. Oskamp, ed. (Hillsdale, NJ: Lawrence Erlbaum. 2000), 93–114.

Preston, Noel. "Exploring Eco-justice: Reframing Ethics and Spirituality in the Context of Globalization." *Occasional Papers* 13 (2001): 1-13.

Qaim, Mahdi Muntazir. *Jesus through the Qur'an and Shi`ite Narrations* (New York: Tahrike Tarsile Qur'an, 2005).

Qureshi, Emran and Michael Anthony Sells, eds, *The New Crusades: Constructing the Muslim Enemy* (New York: Columbia University Press, 2003).

Rahner, Karl. *Foundations of the Christian Faith* (New York: Seabury Press, 1978).

Rilke, Rainer Maria. *The Book of Hours*, Annemarie S. Kidder, trans. (Evanston, IL: Northwestern University Press, 2001).

Roberts, Alexander and Donaldson James, eds. *Ante-Nicene Fathers*, vol. 5 (Grand Rapids: Eerdmans, 1957).

Rosoux, Valérie. "National Identity in France and Germany: from mutual exclusion to negation." *International Negotiation* 2 (2001): 175-198.

Ryrie, Charles. *Dispensationalism* (Chicago: Moody Press, 2007).

Sachedina, Abdulaziz. "Human Viceregency: A Blessing or a Curse?" in *Humanity Before God,* William Schweiker, Michael A. Johnson, and Kevin Jung, eds., (Minneapolis: Augsburg Fortress, 2006).

Said, Edward. *Orientalism* (New York: Pantheon Books, 1978).

Schaff, Philip and Henry Wace. *Nicene and Post-Nicene Fathers*, Series, no. 2, vol. 1. (Grand Rapids: Eerdmans, 1961).

Schrag, Calvin. "Otherness and the Problem of Evil: How Does That Which is Other Become Evil?," *International Journal for Philosophy of Religion* 60: 1/3 (Dec. 2006): 149-156.

Shepherd, William B. "The Diversity of Islamic Thought: Towards a Typology." In *Islamic Thought in the Twentieth Century*, Suha Taji-Farouki and Basheer M. Nafi, eds. (Londn: I.B. Tauris, 2009).

Smith, Jane Idleman and Yvonne Yazbeck Haddad. *The Islamic Understanding of Death and Resurrection* (Albany: State University Press, 1981).

Stiglitz, Joseph. *Making Globalization Work* (New York: W.W. Norton and Co., Inc., 2006).

Stoneman, Richard, trans. and ed. *The Greek Alexander Romance* (New York: Penguin, 1991).

Stoutzenberger, Joseph. *Justice and Peace* (Dubuque, IA: Brown-ROA, 2000).

St. Augustine, *The City of God*, Henry Bettenson, trans. (NY: Penguin, 1984).

Tabrizi, Wali-ud-Din Muhammad bin Abdullah. *Mishkat-Ul-Masabih.* 2 vols. Abdul Hamid Siddiqi, trans. (New Delhi: Kitab Bhavan, 1987).

Taylor, Charles. "The Dialogical Self." In *Rethinking Knowledge: Reflections Across the Disciplines*, Robert F. Goodman and Walter R. Fisher, eds. (Albany: SUNY Press, 1995), 57-66.

Theodosius, Dobzhansky. *Mankind Evolving* (New Haven:Yale University Press, 1962).

Tillich, Paul. *Systematic Theology.* vol. 3 (Chicago: University of Chicago Press, 1963).

Trofimov, Yaroslav. *The Siege of Mecca* (New York: Doubleday, 2007).

Turner, Colin. "Reconsidering Jihad: The Perspective of Bediüzzaman Said Nursi," *Nova Religio* 11: 2 (November 2007): 94-111.

Ünal, Ali. *The Qur'an with Annotated Interpretation in Modern English* (Somerset, NJ: The Light, 2007).

Walls, Jerry, ed. *The Oxford Handbook of Eschatology* (New York: Oxford University Press, 2008).

Winter, Tim, ed. *Classical Islamic Theology* (Cambridge, UK: Cambridge University Press, 2008).

Yates, Michael. *Naming The System: Inequality and Work in the Global Economy* (New York: Monthly Review Press, 2003).

Yahya, Harun. *The End Times and the Mahdi* (Istanbul: Khatoons, 2003).

—. *The Glad Tidings of the Messiah* (Istanbul: Global Publishing, 2004).

Yong, Amos. *Hospitality and the Other. Pentecost, Christian Practices and the Neighbor* (Maryknoll: Orbis Press, 2008).

—. *The Spirit Poured Out On All Flesh. Pentecostalism and the Possibility of Global Theology* (Grand Rapids: Baker, 2005).

Yunus, Muhammad. *Banker to the Poor: Micro-Lending and the Battle against World Poverty* (New York: Public Affairs, 2007).

—. *Creating a World Without Poverty: Social Business and the Future of Capitalism* (New York: Public Affairs, 2007).

CONTRIBUTORS

Dr. David D. Grafton is an Associate Professor of Islamic Studies and Christian-Muslim Relations, and the Director of Graduate Studies of The Lutheran Theological Seminary at Philadelphia. Prior to his appointment at LTSP he served as the Coordinator of Graduate Studies at the Evangelical (Presbyterian) Theological Seminary in Cairo, Director of the Center for Middle East Christianity at the ETSC, and adjunct lecturer in Islamic studies at the Dar Comboni Institute for Arabic and Islamic Studies, Cairo, Egypt. He has a PhD in Islamic Studies from the Center for the Study of Islam and Christian-Muslim Relations, University of Birmingham, England. Dr. Grafton's academic interests focus on Christian-Muslim relationships in the Middle East, 19th and 20th Protestant missionary thought on Islam, 19th and 20th century Islamic social-political thought, as well as the history of the Arab Church. He has provided lectures and seminars on Islam, Middle East Religion and Society, and Christian-Muslim Relations in Jordan, Lebanon, Egypt, Sudan, England, and the United States. He is the author of numerous articles, as well as The Christians of Lebanon: Political Rights in Islamic Law (I.B. Tauris, 2004), and Piety, Politics and Power: Lutherans Encountering Islam in the Middle East (Wipf and Stock, 2009).

Dr. Heon Kim is an Assistant Professor of Philosophy and Religious Studies at East Stroudsburg University of Pennsylvania. He received his doctorate from the Department of Religion, Temple University. His dissertation, "The Nature and Role of Sufism in Contemporary Islam: A Case Study of the Life, Thought and Teachings of Fethullah Gülen," was awarded distinction by his dissertation committee's unanimous vote and is under revision for publication. As the first extensive study of the Sufi (inner and spiritual) dimensions of Gülen's thought and the Gülen movement, it critically explores the possibilities and limitations of Sufism as an alternative to Islamic fundamentalist movements and as a dialogical bridge between Islam and other religions. Dr. Kim received his B.A. in Arabic Language from Hankuk University of Foreign Studies, Seoul, South Korea. He subsequently studied Arabic and Islamic theology for several years at Al-Azhar University, Cairo, Egypt. His academic career continued at Marmara University in Istanbul, Turkey, where he obtained

an M.A. degree in Islamic Philosophy. Dr. Kim is the author of Din
Değiştirmenin Entellectual Arka Planı (Intellectual Background of Religious
Conversion), which was published in Turkish and is in translation into
English. With a series of conference presentations and publication projects,
he is currently working on Sufi concept of humanism, its implications for
the globalized humanity, and the transformation of a regional Sufism into
global Sufism. His research interests range from "Sufism and Islamic
Spirituality," "Islamic Religious Experience," "Muslim Minority and
Gender Issues," to "Comparative Religions: Islam and East Asian
Religious Traditions," "Inter-religious Dialogue" and "Humanism in Islam
and other religious traditions."

Dr. Karina Korostelina is an Associate Professor at the Institute for
Conflict Analysis and Resolution, GMU and a Fellow of the European
Research Center of Migration and Ethnic Relation (ERCOMER). She is a
leading experts on identity-based conflicts, ethnic conflicts, the
relationships between Muslim and non-Muslim populations, conflict
resolution and peacebuilding. She has been Fulbright New Century
Scholar and a Regional Scholar at the Kennan Institute She has received
grants from the MacArthur Foundation, Soros Foundation, the United
State Institute of Peace, US National Academy of Education, Spenser
Foundation, Bureau of Educational and Cultural Affairs of USDS, USAID,
INTAS, IREX, and Council of Europe. Among her books are: The social
identity and Conflict (2007); Structure and Dynamics of Social Identity
(2003). She is an editor of Identity, Morality and Threat (2006) and
Interethnic Coexistence in the Crimea: The Ways of Achievement (2002).

Dr. Jon Pahl is Professor of the History of Christianity in North America
and Director of MA Programs for The Lutheran Theological Seminary at
Philadelphia, and has been Visiting Professor of Religion at Temple
University and Princeton University. Dr. Pahl received his Ph.D. from the
University of Chicago Divinity School. He has published numerous
articles and columns, and has authored or edited seven books, including
Shopping Malls and Other Sacred Spaces, and, most recently, Empire of
Sacrifice: The Religious Origins of American Violence (NYU Press). Jon
has enjoyed speaking with audiences from Ankara, Turkey to Anaheim,
California, has been interviewed on the BBC and other media outlets, and
was featured in a documentary film, Malls R Us, which had its world
premiere at the Museum of Modern Art in New York City. Jon lives with
his wife, Lisa, and their three children near Swarthmore, PA, where he

enjoys sports, gardening, and playing the saxophone with his jazz and rhythm and blues band, "The Groove Daemons."

Dr. John Raines is a Professor of Religion at Temple University. In 2004 he was voted "Professor of the Year" by the Honors Program and in 2006 was awarded The Lindbeck "Outstanding Teacher Award." For many years he was the Chair of the Board of The Religious Consultation on Population, Reproductive Health and Ethics. He has written many books and articles, among them Modern Work And Human Meaning (1986) and The Justice Men Owe Women (2002). Raines has been a Fulbright Research Fellow in Malaysia and a Fulbright Teaching Fellow in Indonesia and has received grants promoting educational exchanges with The Center for Religious and Cross-Cultural Studies at Gadjah Mada University in Indonesia from The U.S. Institute of Peace, The Henry Luce Foundation, The Fulbright Program and The John Templeton Foundation. Raines was active in the Civil Rights Movement in the 1960s and was several times jailed for his activities in the south. He refers to this as "his second education" where he learned "what power looks like when you are outside of power and viewed as its enemy." His most recent research and publications have concerned the affects of global capitalism upon the world's food system and why it is that when we let "food follow money" we end up with 2 billion people suffering from severe food insecurity when there is adequate agricultural productive capacity to feed and feed well all 6 and ½ billion now inhabiting the earth. Raines is married to Bonnie Muir Raines, has four children and seven grandchildren, and lives in Center City Philadelphia. He is an ordained United Methodist clergy person.

Dr. Margaret J. Rausch received her MA in Middle Eastern History from Ohio State University and PhD in Islamic Studies from the Free University of Berlin, where she taught until 2001, followed by appointments in Religious Studies at the University of Kansas and Rockhurst University. Her research interests encompass Muslim women's religious authority and ritual participation, and self-refashioning and affect in Sufi, Neo-Sufi and Islamic reform initiatives. She has conducted fieldwork in Morocco, Egypt, Tajikistan and the US and received fellowships from the American Council of Learned Societies, American Institute for Maghrib Studies and Fulbright-Hays. Her publications include *Bodies, Boundaries and Spirit Possession. Moroccan Women and the Revision of Tradition* (Transcript Verlag, 2001) and Moroccan Women Mosque Preachers and Spiritual Guides: Publicizing and Negotiating Women's Religious Authority. In H.

Kalmbach and M. Bano (eds), *Women, Leadership and Mosques* (Brill, 2011). She is currently revising her book manuscript *Berber Women's Rituals and Islamic Reform in Southwestern Morocco: Language, Body and Affect.*

Dr. Ori Z. Soltes is Goldman Professorial Lecturer in Theology and Fine Arts at Georgetown University, and former Director and Curator of the B'nai B'rith Klutznick National Jewish Museum in Washington, DC, where he curated over 80 exhibitions. He has taught and lectured in 23 other universities and museums throughout the country and overseas, on subjects ranging from the Arab-Israeli conflict to The Body in Ancient Art. Professor Soltes is the author of over 180 articles, exhibition catalogues, essays and books on a wide range of topics, including Our Sacred Signs: How Christian, Jewish and Muslim Art Draw from the Same Source, (Westview, 2005); Searching for Oneness: Mysticism in the Jewish, Christian and Muslim Traditions (Rowman and Littlefield, 2008); and Untangling the Web: Why the Middle East is a Mess and Always Was (Bartleby, 2010). He is currently writing a book relating the thought of Fetulleh Gülen to that of Jellaludin Rumi.

Dr. Joseph Stoutzenberger is Professor of Religious Studies at Holy Family University in Philadelphia, Pennsylvania. He has a Master's Degree in Religious Education from Loyola University, Chicago, and an M.A. and Ph. D. in Religion from Temple University. He is the author of numerous books, including The Christian Call to Justice and Peace (St. Mary's Press), Justice and Peace (Harcourt Religion Publishers), and The Human Quest for God: An Overview of World Religions (Twenty-Third Publications). He has also contributed to Interfaith Dialogue at the Grass Roots, published by Ecumenical Press.

Dr. Walter H. Wagner is adjunct faculty at Moravian Theological Seminary (Bethlehem, PA) and the Lutheran Theological Seminary, Philadelphia. He is an ordained Lutheran pastor (ELCA), retired from parish ministry. He has taught at California, Lutheran College, Upsala College and Muhlenberg College, and served as the director for theological education of the Lutheran Church in America. He is the author of a number of articles on early church history and Islam as well as Opening the Qur'an. Introducing Islam's Holy Book (Notre Dame Press); After the Apostles. Christianity in the Second Century (Fortress Press); and The Zinzendorf-Muhlenberg Encounter: A Controversy Seeking Understanding (Moravian Historical Society). He holds the B.A. (Gettysburg

College), M.Div. (Lutheran Theological Seminary), M.A. (Princeton Theological Seminary) and Ph.D. (Drew University). He has been involved in ecumenical and inter-religious activities and programs for many years.

INDEX